GOD IN EDUCATION

THE ROCKWELL LECTURES
DELIVERED AT THE RICE INSTITUTE

Other Books by the Same Author

WORLD CHRISTIANITY: YESTERDAY, TODAY AND TOMORROW

THEY FOUND THE CHURCH THERE

EAST INDIES DISCOVERIES

WHAT *IS* THE CHURCH DOING?

REALITY AND RELIGION (Hazen Series)

METHODISM'S WORLD MISSION

FOR THE HEALING OF THE NATIONS: IMPRESSIONS OF CHRISTIANITY
AROUND THE WORLD

GOD IN THESE TIMES

THE PLAIN MAN SEEKS FOR GOD

IN QUEST OF LIFE'S MEANING

Edited by Henry P. Van Dusen

THE CHRISTIAN ANSWER

LIBERAL THEOLOGY: AN APPRAISAL
(with David E. Roberts)

CHURCH AND STATE IN THE MODERN WORLD

THE CHURCH THROUGH HALF A CENTURY
(with Samuel McCrea Cavert)

VENTURES IN BELIEF

THE STORY OF JESUS
(with Thomas W. Graham)

GOD
IN
EDUCATION

GOD IN EDUCATION

A
TRACT FOR THE TIMES

BY
HENRY P. VAN DUSEN

NEW YORK
CHARLES SCRIBNER'S SONS
1951

To the Memory of
MY FATHER
GEORGE RICHSTEIN VAN DUSEN
1857–1916
Who Taught Me
Reverence for Truth
Respect for Law
The Duty of Eternal Vigilance
in defense of both
Truth and Justice

PREFACE

THESE few pages attempt to set forth a vast panorama on a very small canvas. Inevitably, the strokes are broad and the outlines sharp; there is a deliberate disregard of delicate shadings and precise detail. A critic may well protest that the trees have been neglected in preoccupation with the woods. That is intentional. There is a characteristically paradoxical but pregnant saying of G. K. Chesterton, "The only important thing about knowing the truth is to know the important truth." In these brief chapters, I have tried to set forth what I believe to be the most important single truth about *education*. Both the aim and the limitations of the book are hinted in the subtitle, "A Tract for the Times." On the one hand, it makes no pretense to balanced completeness but is in the literal sense "occasional" (or, as the current phrase has it, "existential"). On the other hand, it intends to deal with matters of clamant urgency for today.

There is no dearth of recent writing on the general subject of education and religion. On the contrary, one of the most significant and heartening signs of the times is the greatly increased attention within the last decade to the place of religion in education. This has borne concrete results both in the inauguration of new departments and courses in religion in many colleges and universities and in a welcome spate of essays, pamphlets and books in this field. Some of the more valuable of these are mentioned in the Bibliography.

But virtually all of these writings deal with "religion" as a special subject or interest, and discuss principally such topics as the place of a department of religion or religious courses within the curriculum, the impregnation of other courses with religious teaching or outlook, the role of college chapel, the stimulation of religious interest and activity among faculty members, etc. With a single exception, none of them, so far as I am aware, attempts to face what must be for education both the basic and the final issue—the issue of ultimate Truth, the bearing of the *truth*, for which religion stands, on the philosophy and structure of education as a whole; that is, what if any is the meaning for educational theory and practice of the *recognition of God*.

How are we to account for this neglect of the main issue in recent discussions in this area? It cannot be because many of those who have written so admirably were unaware of it. Is the true explanation, perhaps, to be found in the fact that, *if this issue is really faced*, its implications for the underlying and controlling philosophy and structure of higher education are so radical that no hope of their acceptance can be entertained? But, surely, our primary loyalty is to *Truth*. I have sought to present what I conceive to be the central issue with some of its corollaries, whatever the chances of their adoption.

I say none of these writings deals thoroughly with the central issue, *with a single exception*. Since my chapters were completed in first draft, there has come into my hands a book which does wrestle directly and fearlessly with precisely this basic and ultimate issue, and in almost exactly the perspective which I am concerned to hold. This is Sir Walter Moberley's *The Crisis in the University*, regarded by many others as well as by myself as the most important single work on education written in this century. The position Sir Walter develops is so closely parallel to the main argument of my chapters that I cannot forego the insertion of some quotations from his book.

But what he has written has confirmed, not formed, my own thinking.

In the spring of 1947, I gave one of the Pitcairn-Crabbe lectures at the University of Pittsburgh on "Religion and Education," which subsequently appeared in *Modern Education and Human Values* published by the University of Pittsburgh Press. The invitation to give the Rockwell Lectures at the Rice Institute, Houston, Texas, in the spring of 1950 offered an opportunity to expand the thesis of the single lecture into this small volume. I am indebted to the University of Pittsburgh Press for consent to this expansion, and to the Officers, Faculty, and Students of the Rice Institute for surpassingly gracious and appreciative hospitality. Because of the paramount importance of RELIGION IN PUBLIC EDUCATION in the United States at the present time, I have added a brief essay on that subject.

Professors F. Ernest Johnson and Clarence P. Shedd have kindly given me the benefit of their comments on the entire manuscript, and my former teacher, Professor-emeritus Edwin S. Corwin of Princeton, has scrutinized the essay on RELIGION IN PUBLIC EDUCATION which is, in considerable part, indebted to his own writing on this topic.

H. P. V. D.

Union Theological Seminary
New York
February 18, 1951

CONTENTS

CHAPTER THREE

PROSPECT: WHICH WAY AHEAD?

IN SUMMARY

RELIGION IN PUBLIC EDUCATION

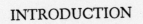

INTRODUCTION

INTRODUCTION

THESE are days which are testing to the last limit the optimism and hope of every intelligent and informed person. We live in a world which threatens to break in pieces under our eyes.

Through all the current diagnoses of civilization's sickness, which shadows most men's minds with apprehension and some with desperation, there runs a single note, like a persistent and monotonous *motif*. So obvious is it that we accept it as self-evident. So familiar is it that it stirs our imaginations no more than the ticking of a clock. *The knowledge and skills of Modern Civilization have outrun the moral and spiritual resources for their direction and control.* In this land of plenty, glutted with wealth, we lack the essential ethical currency for its use, and so we are threatened with cultural bankruptcy.

From the considered statements of national leaders, one may choose almost at random for illustrations of this consensus. Virtually all are saying essentially the same thing, in only slightly variant phrasing, with wearisome reiteration. At the dedication of the great Palomar Observatory, Dr. Raymond B. Fosdick focused his dedicatory address in these words:

> *"Knowledge is not enough. . . . Unless we can anchor our knowledge to moral foundations, the ultimate result will be dust and ashes. . . . The towering enemy of man is not his science but his moral inadequacy."*

17

Governor Dewey, accepting nomination for the Presidency of the United States, declared:

> *"Our problem is within ourselves. We have found the means to blow the world, physically, apart. Spiritually, we have yet to find the means to put together the world's broken pieces."*

The Hon. John Foster Dulles insists:

> *"Men's ability to control the physical depends upon the moral. . . . There is no short cut. It is not possible by a stroke of the pen to make up for accumulated moral deficiencies."*

The head of the Armed Forces, General Omar N. Bradley, recently declared:

> *"Humanity is in danger of being trapped in this world by its moral adolescence. Our knowledge of science has already outstripped our capacity to control it.*
>
> *"We have too many men of science; too few men of God. We have grasped the mystery of the atom and rejected the Sermon on the Mount. Man is stumbling blindly through a spiritual darkness while toying with the precarious secrets of life and death.*
>
> *"The world has achieved brilliance without wisdom, power without conscience. Ours is a world of nuclear giants and ethical infants."*

All men agree. The imperative need of today, overshadowing all other unnumbered and urgent needs, is firmer and stronger character, higher integrity, larger spiritual vision, unimpeachable and unshakable fidelity, what one of our foremost statesmen keeps pleading for—*"a righteous and dynamic faith."*

But it has been given to another military leader to sum the whole matter up in five words. Standing on the deck of the Battleship *Missouri* on V-J Day, General Douglas MacArthur put the heart of what he had to say, heard round the world, in this pithy sentence:

"Our problem is basically theological."

That is, it is in the area of men's fundamental conviction about the nature of their world, and the Power which rules it, themselves, and their history.

Inevitably, thoughtful persons are turning with new attention toward that factor which, among the multifarious interests of humanity, has traditionally specialized in supplying precisely these lacks, which deals explicitly with the question of God. They ask with a new wistfulness: What help if any at the crucial point of this nation's, the world's, need may reasonably be expected, in the days ahead, from religion?

In these pages, we are to be occupied with only one aspect of that question—the place of *God in education.* But we shall miss the significance of our specific topic unless we place it, and hold it firmly, within the wider context. Moreover, because we are dealing with the fundamental character of contemporary civilization, we shall foreshorten perspective unless our situation today is seen in the setting of the historic developments of which it is the outcome. For this reason, I offer no apology for centering our attention at the outset on "THE LARGER BACKGROUND."

RETROSPECT: THE LARGER BACKGROUND

CHAPTER ONE

RETROSPECT:
THE LARGER BACKGROUND

BY UNIVERSAL acknowledgment, the foremost Christian statesman of the first half of this century was the late William Temple, Archbishop of Canterbury. Temple's towering eminence lay in the fact that in him superb natural gifts of mind and heart, illumined and disciplined by solid learning and wide experience, were permeated and ennobled by deep spirituality and unaffected simplicity. All this, speaking with a perception of the highest powers wholly devoted to truth, places him also in the front rank of theologians. Probably his greatest theological writing is to be found in his Gifford Lectures, *Nature, Man and God*, which stand in the forefront of that great series, the most distinguished in the field of religion in the English-speaking world.

Early in this volume, Temple opens a masterly review of the development of modern thought with this semi-facetious but profound remark:

"If I were asked what was the most disastrous moment in the history of Europe I should be strongly tempted to answer that it was that period of leisure when René Descartes, having no claims to meet, remained for a whole day 'shut up alone in a stove.' " [1]

[1] *Nature, Man and God*, p. 57. Copyright by The Macmillan Company and used with their permission.

"Surely," we are tempted to rejoin, "such decisive importance can hardly be attributed to any individual, however influential." But Descartes is generally recognized as "the Father of Modern Thought." Perhaps more than any other philosopher, he determined the issues, and the terms for their resolution, which have preoccupied the ablest thinkers down to our own day. Moreover, his significance, especially for our interest, lies less in his direct influence than in his representative character, less in the fact that he was an architect of the Modern Mind than in the fact that he was, to such a remarkable degree, its symbol. As Temple goes on to say:

> "That many of our worst troubles, not only in philosophy but also in politics and economics, with all that this means for human happiness or misery, are closely associated with the habit of thought then established I cannot doubt." [2]

Descartes was one of those rare figures who anticipated in his own outlook trends of thought which were to achieve currency and dominance only in later decades or even centuries. If we give somewhat extended attention to Descartes, it is because we can discover in him, as precursor of the Modern Age, some of its most distinctive and determinative characteristics.

II

Descartes' personal dilemma, and his way out of it, are a familiar tale. Intense study, especially in mathematics, had embogged the youthful mind of twenty-three in complete scepticism. "I found myself," he declared, "with so many doubts and errors that it seemed to me that the effort to instruct myself had no effect other than the increasing discovery of my own ignorance." [3] On the other hand, "I was delighted

[2] *Ibid.*
[3] This, and the quotations which follow, are from *Discourse on Method.*

with Mathematics," he continues, "because of the certainty of its demonstrations and the evidence of its reasoning." The absolute precision of mathematics thus furnished him with an exacting standard for truth which no generally accepted facts of nature or history could fully meet; in comparison, "the writings of the ancient moralists . . . are built on nothing but sand or mud." Thus Descartes' mind could rest satisfied with nothing less than mathematical certainty; but such certitude appeared beyond his reach. "I thought it necessary for me . . . to reject as absolutely false everything as to which I could imagine the least ground of doubt." He struggled in a morass of unrelieved skepticism.

It was in this mood of utter agnosticism and despair that Descartes resolved to shut himself off completely—from all tradition, all that had come down to him from the past; from all association with his fellow men, all light to be derived from his contemporaries; even, so far as possible, from all contact with the external world with its baffling imprecision and change ("I resolved to assume that everything that ever entered my mind was no more true than the illusions of my dreams," he reports)—and, in undisturbed isolation, to search his own interior thoughts for ideas so clear, so coercive, so inescapable, that they at least could not possibly be questioned. "I formed one day the resolution to study within myself . . . and, fortunately, having no cares or passions to trouble me, I spent the whole day shut up alone in a stove-heated room." This was the setting for his period of solitary reflection which the Archbishop of Canterbury suggests may have been the most disastrous moment in the history of Europe.

Descartes' first task was to define a *method* of truth-discovery in which he might place fullest confidence:

1. "To accept nothing as true which I did not clearly know to be so . . . nothing more than what was pre-

sented to my mind so clearly and distinctly that I could have no occasion to doubt it."

2. "To divide up every difficulty into as many parts as possible."

3. "To carry on my reflections in an orderly manner, beginning with the most simple and easiest to understand, in order to rise little by little."

4. "To make enumerations so complete, and reviews so comprehensive, that I should be certain of having omitted nothing."

With a firm hold upon these principles of procedure, Descartes set himself to examine the contents of his own mind in search of one idea, so clear, distinct, indisputable that he could not elude its compulsion. Ultimately, he came upon an idea which fulfilled his specifications. It was the *idea of himself*—not, to be sure, of himself as a total personality with body and brain and emotions, but of himself as *a mind thinking*. "*Je pense, donc je suis. Cogito; ergo sum,*" he cried to himself. "I think; there is someone here thinking. Therefore, I am; I exist." "From that I knew that I was a substance the whole essence or nature of which is to think . . . so that this 'me' is entirely distinct from body." This idea he triumphantly accepted "as the first principle of the Philosophy for which I was seeking."

Pursuing his exercise in introspection further, he next fastened upon the *idea of a Perfect Being*. This, likewise, was to him an idea so clear, so compelling that it could not be doubted. Moreover, it was so obviously not of his origination that it must have been lodged in his mind by "a Nature . . . more perfect than mine could be." Thus, he now felt assured of the existence of God; "there was necessarily some other more perfect Being on which I depended, or from which I acquired all that I had."

From these two primal certainties—himself as a mind *and* God—he moved on to *assume* the reality of his own body, of Nature, of *the external world*. He felt confident that the Perfect Deity whose existence he had established as beyond dispute would not allow him to be deceived in the overwhelming *impression* that there was a physical world beyond his own thinking, including the physiological organism which housed his mind. But this was merely an inference from the trustworthiness of God. Descartes could thus affirm three realities— *himself, God, Nature*—God being the link between the other two. On the basis of this trialistic certitude, he sought to build up all knowledge.

III

I have no doubt that Descartes' somewhat fantastic ruminations seem at far remove from our times, from our interests, and more particularly from our topic. I have suggested that he is important only partly because of his direct influence upon the development of thought in the three centuries since, but much more as a forerunner and representative of the Modern Mind. As we might expect, there is no place where the characteristic features of the modern outlook find clearer expression than in our academic communities, in the seats of scholarship and learning. Consider four of these features, first as they were anticipated in the mind of René Descartes, and then as we are familiar with them, largely unchallenged assumptions in contemporary educational philosophy and practice:

1. First of all, the *perspective* which Descartes chose for his intellectual quest was solitude—the individual mind in isolation from Nature, from history, from society. Here is a major philosophic source-spring of the *Individualism* which has been such a marked, and latterly often-remarked, feature

of the Modern Period. Again, Descartes was resolved to discover secure truth within his own mind, without conscious
dependence upon the external world. This is the root premise
of all *Rationalism, Subjectivism* and *Intellectualism.* The mar-
riage of *Individualism* and *Intellectualism,* the twin basic features of the Cartesian perspective, has bred the *Egocentrism,*
the *Anthropocentrism* of Modern Man, certainly Modern
Man as scholar.

René Descartes himself was the most extreme of individ-
ualists and intellectualists. The picture of the youthful mathematical philosopher, shut up within his solitary retreat—seemingly independent of Nature, and deliberately divorced from
responsible relations with his fellow men with all their annoy-
ances, their obligations, their frustrations, but also with their
enrichments, their satisfactions, their fulfillments (as Temple
suggests, "with no claims to meet")—is the perfect prototype
of the modern self-centered and self-satisfied individualist.
Descartes' chosen stance was the attempt to create ideal conditions for the Rationalist-Individualist enterprise.

The dominance of this perspective within modern thought
requires no proof. For illustration we do not need to look
beyond the world of learning—the typical individualism of
academicians, often shielded from demanding social relation-
ships and obligations, cherishing a life of privileged security
and exemption from public duties and irritations. Or the
world of popular religion with its dictum that "religion is
what a man does with his own solitariness," its preference for
a purely individual religion which each person may develop
for himself ("every man his own theologian"), recognizing
no dependence upon others, and acknowledging no account-
ability for the bearing of one's faith upon the great and press-
ing issues of society. But a similar ideal has lured almost every
typical son of the modern day; he has coveted an existence of
unfettered personal independence and self-determination, to

be made possible for him through the acquisition of wealth.

Actually, Descartes' imagined isolation was spurious; it was belied by more acute attention to the facts. Even in his comfortable retreat, he was divorced from neither Nature nor society. There were cracks in that stove through which air penetrated to his lungs. Had this supply of ozone been for two moments withdrawn, or had a capricious Sovereign of despised physical Nature wished to rebuke his disdain by altering momentarily the complex of natural law in accordance with which our bodies live, Descartes' mind would have ceased its self-important cogitation like a pleasant dream under the stern summons of an alarm-clock. He would have been rudely disabused of his delusion that he was "a substance the whole essence or nature of which is to think . . . so that this 'me' is entirely distinct from body." Moreover, all the while the solitary thinker was reveling in self-absorbed speculation, some faithful cook was wrestling with pots and pans for his supper, and the vast network of society's organism was toiling through its accustomed routine to make possible his privileged ruminations.

Descartes' perspective was fundamentally false. So, likewise, is the modern point of view in the measure that it perpetuates Individualism and Intellectualism. Thought divorced from its dependence upon body, upon Nature, is a fanciful abstraction; therefore, no safe guide to knowledge of Reality. Man divorced from dependence upon his fellows, upon Society, is a self-deceived abstraction; therefore, no safe guide for the direction of human affairs. Yet this is the perspective which has dominated much of modern education.

2. Descartes assumed that every seeker after truth should begin his quest *de novo*, without reference to previous discoveries. Note how that assumption, likewise, conditions the intellectual enterprise in our own day, as illustrated in our

academic communities. What self-respecting student has not passed through the momentous episode, traditionally in sophomore year in college but today more probably in high school, when he has felt duty-bound to follow in Descartes' footsteps, to divest himself of every inherited belief, every common-sense assumption, and, with no conscious presuppositions, to set forth upon his personal quest for truth? In the wider corporate scene, this is the very essence of *Modernism*—disdain of the wisdom of the past, assumption of the authority of the latest: the cult of contemporaneity.

In espousing this approach, Modern Man has proclaimed himself a devotee of scientific method. In fact, this is the direct obverse of true scientific method. Every scientist begins his labors with shelves crowded with the accumulated and tested discoveries of his predecessors. He assumes them correct unless and until they are proven mistaken, although he intends to reverify their validity repeatedly. He aims to build upon and go beyond the achievements of earlier investigators to new discoveries made possible only because of the funded wisdom of the centuries. Moreover, as Eddington has pointed out, new scientific truth seldom discredits and discards earlier scientific beliefs. More characteristically, it embraces them and sets them within a wider and truer context—very much as, in putting together a jig-saw puzzle, parts of the picture already pieced together are incorporated within a larger whole; a patch of blue, originally diagnosed as a parasol, is next thought to be a bit of lake, but finally takes its true place within the expanse of the Heavens.[4]

3. Descartes was a devotee of *mathematics*. As we have said, his mind could rest satisfied only with conclusions sustained

[4] A. S. Eddington, *The Nature of the Physical World*, p. 325. "Scientific discovery is like the fitting together of the pieces of a great jig-saw puzzle; a revolution of science does not mean that the pieces already arranged and interlocked have to be dispersed; it means that in fitting on fresh pieces we have had to revise our impression of what the puzzle-picture is going to be like."

by the absolute precision and finality of mathematics. In this objective, he was truly the precursor of Modern Science. And it is a platitude that the most important key to the Modern World, both its life and its thought, has been the dominance of science, a fact for which we may coin the word "*Scientism.*" The great preoccupation of Modern Thought has been to agree upon the meaning of science for men's outlook. The main issues of debate have sprung from seeming conflicts between the findings of science and previously accepted assumptions. The ruling purpose, often unconscious, of the regnant philosophies has been to develop a view of things thoroughly harmonious with the outlook and conclusions of science, a "scientific philosophy."

Lest there be a moment's suspicion that we are tempted to deprecate the advance of science or to rouse the corpse of the old science-religion controversy, let us acknowledge at once and in one sweeping phrase our unqualified acceptance of the tested results of Modern Science and our immeasurable debt to science's enrichment of human existence. We are merely concerned to note the larger impact of science upon Modern Thought and Modern Life. That impact has been threefold—through the *goal* of science, through the *methodology* of science, and through the more general *point-of-view* of science, what we may call the *scientific outlook.*

Following Descartes, the *aim* of every science has been an exactitude and objectivity and finality modeled upon mathematics; more than that, the reduction of its data to mathematical symbols. But such mathematical precision can deal only with unalterable relations; that is to say, with mechanical relations; that is, upon the assumption of mechanism. Such mechanism has been the avowed or covert presupposition of every science which sought mathematical finality. One of the most authoritative interpreters of the "New Psychology" puts the necessity of this assumption for a scientific account of the operations of the human soul with commendable bluntness:

"We may admit, perhaps, that there is at present less evidence for the hypothesis of universal determinism in the psychical than there is in the physical sphere, but there is certainly enough to make it a reasonable working hypothesis, and *without such a hypothesis we cannot proceed at all.* . . . Without the hypothesis of universal determination, practical life would be impossible, physical science would be impossible, and psychology would be impossible." [5]

This goal has determined the *method* of science—*analysis, description, classification, generalization*—the method so clearly foreshadowed by Descartes in his four-point program, the familiar technique of the scientific laboratory. The truth supremely prized is that which can be caught within the meshes of this particular net—those facts which admit of complete analysis and classification as instances of a general type. Data which elude this net tend to be disregarded, or, in any event, reduced to secondary importance.

Goal and method created the more general but also more pervasive influence of science upon all Modern Thought through what may be called the *scientific outlook.* Inevitably, this outlook focused attention upon those aspects of human experience and reality with which science was prepared most readily to deal, to the denial or neglect of other aspects which escape scientific instruments. That means a concentration upon the *general* rather than the *individual,* the *universal* rather than the *particular,* the *elementary* rather than the *mature* (witness the preoccupation of experimental psychology, especially in its early stages, with rats, guinea-pigs, and infants), the *uniform* rather than the *unique,* the *familiar* rather than the *original,* the *quantitative* rather than the *quali-*

[5] A. G. Tansley, *The New Psychology,* p. 18. Italics mine. Dr. Ernest Johnson rightly reminds me that Tansley's viewpoint would be disavowed by many of the ablest *contemporary* scientists.

tative, the *commonplace* rather than the *delicate*, the *rare*, the *meaningful*, the *profound*. In brief, it nurtures a perspective directly antipodal to that which the nobler thinkers of the ages had made their own; and a preoccupation with data at precisely the opposite pole from those which the great philosophies, not to speak of art and religion, had learned to recognize as most significant.

Here is the real nub of the century-long tension between science and religion. As Professor Hoffding wrote some years ago:

> "It is not so much the results at which science is arriving, or has arrived, which bring about the quarrel between science and religion, and condition the religious problem; but rather the whole trend of ideas, the entire habit of mind which empirical science has fostered in those who have developed under its influence."

But it is of the highest importance to realize that in its struggle against the dominance of the "scientific outlook," religion was not battling for itself only. Although this has not always been recognized, the interests of religion were no less the concern of the poets, the artists, the lovers, and the devotees of every aspect of human experience in which worth attaches to richness and depth, to variety and originality and individuality. Speaking of the resistance of the Romantic poets, Wordsworth in particular, to the dominance of the prevailing mechanistic assumptions, Whitehead declares:

> "In the nineteenth century, some of the deeper thinkers among the theologians and philosophers were muddled thinkers. . . .
> "Wordsworth in his whole being expresses a conscious reaction against the mentality (which) . . . means nothing less than the acceptance of the scientific ideas at their

full value. Wordsworth was not bothered by any intellectual antagonism. What moved him was moral repulsion. He felt that something had been left out, and that what had been left out comprised everything that was most important. . . .

"The romantic reaction was a protest on behalf of value." [6]

4. Lastly, Descartes distinguished sharply "thought" (*res cogitans*) from "matter" (*res extensa*), and was unable to solve the relation between the *ideas* of Nature in his own mind and the *reality* of the external world, or even between his own mind of whose existence he felt certain through direct intuition and his body whose existence he could only infer, save by appeal to the trustworthiness of God who surely would not mislead him in his impression that there was an external world and that his mind inhabited a body.

Thus Descartes bequeathed to his successors a world riven into two disparate and unrelated realms—spirit and matter, mind and body. In direct influence upon subsequent thought, this was probably Descartes' most determinative legacy. *Dualism* of one kind or another is the most persistent thread through all speculation since.

However, later thinkers could not rest satisfied in the resolution of the dilemma by appeal to Deity. God as connecting-link tended to drop out. Some, like Spinoza, proposed to interpret mind and body as two sides of a shield, coordinate aspects of some mysterious, indefinable third Substance which is the true reality of which both mind and body are appearances; this is *Pantheism*. Others, for example Malebranche and Berkeley, sought to absorb matter into mind or spirit and recognize only the latter as real; this is metaphysical *Idealism*. Still others, such as Hobbes and Hume, attempted

[6] A. N. Whitehead, *Science and the Modern World*, Ch. V.

the opposite resolution—the reduction of thought to a function of the physical organism; in contemporary psychology this "solution" of the dilemma has been worked out with unabashed consistency as thorough-going *Materialism.*

The major line of development, however, passes through the greatest of the post-Cartesians, Immanuel Kant. Kant reformulated the Cartesian dilemma as the dualism of *noumena* and *phenomena*, reality as it actually is *and* reality as it appears to us. The former, reality as it truly is, we can never reach through the ordinary processes of truth-discovery but only through moral insight, which Kant called "faith." On the other hand, the realm of appearances, things as they seem to us to be, is the specific zone in which science works and in which science is authoritative.

But this Kantian dualism has suffered another radical reformulation which Kant little anticipated and almost certainly would have deplored. The distinction between phenomena and noumena has become the much more familiar (to us) distinction between facts and values, between the realm of science *and* the realm of art and religion; more recently between the *secular* and the *spiritual*. To Kant it was the distinction between the realm of phenomenal appearances of which we may have "scientific knowledge" but no certainty, and the realm of true reality of which we may have no scientific *knowledge* but such practical certainty as men may live by. Under the alchemy of modern thought, we now confront the contrast between the world of facts of which science gives us the only genuine knowledge we may have, and the realm of values which is conceded no validity beyond our own appreciations and feelings. What to Kant was only appearance and therefore of negligible ultimate importance has become for us the basis of the only certainty we possess; what was for Kant the supremely important key to reality—the insights achieved through moral experience—has become for us the insecure realm of subjective valuations. The roles are reversed. Science, formerly merely useful interpreter of phenomenal appearances, is now hailed as our sole guide to truth; while the moral consciousness, to Kant our one safe pilot to Ultimate Reality, struggles to establish its right to tell us what we ought and ought not to do.

The history of human thought knows no more pathetic paradox than the contrast between the intended effect and the actual effect of the thought of these two great men, René Descartes and Immanuel Kant, upon that interest which lay closest to the heart of each, *belief in God*. To the end of his days, Descartes remained not only a firm believer in God but a devout Roman Catholic.

> "I honoured our Theology and aspired as much as any-one to reach to heaven, but having learned to regard it as a most highly assured fact that the road is not less open to the most ignorant than to the most learned, and that the revealed truths which conduct thither are quite above our intelligence, I should not have dared to submit them to the feebleness of my reasonings; and I thought that, in order to undertake to examine them and succeed in so doing, it was necessary to have some extraordinary assistance from above and to be more than a mere man." [7]

His religious beliefs he thus accepted on the authority of revelation by faith, although, as already pointed out, he also intended to prove philosophically the existence of God as beyond dispute. In his religion, Descartes looked out toward the past, toward an age which was already dying. In his scientific and philosophic theories, he was the precursor of the age aborning. Inevitably, the latter triumphed over the former. As his philosophical *tour de force*—God as connecting-link between mind and body—tended to disappear in the subsequent

[7] *Discourse on Method*, Part I, p. 7.

development, so did his pious acceptance of revealed truth. All unwittingly, he became the parent of much modern philosophical materialism and unbelief.

A closely parallel fate overtook Kant's intentions. He declared that his purpose was "to abolish knowledge in order to make room for faith." The outcome has been almost exactly the reverse of his intention. That part of human thought to which he gave the word "knowledge"—the elements in experience suitable for scientific treatment—has won increasing reverence as the only proper material for philosophical speculation; and its interpreter, science, has received increasing recognition as the only sure guide to truth. That part of truth to which, in Kant's view, moral insight alone could give access has been accorded diminishing metaphysical significance; and our guide thereto, "faith," has become increasingly suspect, tainted with the opprobrium of "wishful thinking." [8]

Both Descartes and Kant, unintentionally, proved to be subverters rather than guardians of religion because each philosopher sought to preserve faith in a realm apart from that to which the livest energies of modern thinking have been directed—Descartes, through distinguishing sharply the truths of science from the truths of revelation, releasing the former from concern with ultimate issues and buttressing the latter by the dubious authority of Roman Catholic dogma; Kant, by dichotomizing *his* world into the realm of familiar experience and the realm of noumenal reality, assigning the former to science's dicta and restricting our apprehension of ultimate truths to the deliveries of moral insight. But in an age increasingly skeptical of special revelation and suspicious of the trustworthiness of personal intuition, an age more and more preoccupied with the triumphs of science in mastering *this* world of familiar experience and putting it to the service of

[8] This aspect of Kant's teaching and influence is worked out more fully in the author's *The Plain Man Seeks for God*, pp. 37–55.

man's security and comfort and pleasure, it was inevitable
that a progressively larger sovereignty should be exerted by
scientific presuppositions, viewpoints and conclusions, while
religious belief, confined to a realm immune to scientific scru-
tiny and supported by suspect sanctions, should suffer a deep-
ening eclipse.

Descartes' and Kant's mistake was in their basic premise—
radical dualism, the dualism which, in our day, appears most
clearly as the divorce of the "sacred" from the "secular." God,
if He exists at all, must be the Sovereign of *all* Reality. He
must be so discerned. And He must be so confessed. Therefore, the truth concerning Him, as men can best apprehend
it, must be, *a fortiori*, the controlling principle of all knowledge and of that enterprise supremely consecrated to the
achievement, interpretation and transmission of knowledge—
education.

IV

Individualism, Intellectualism, Modernism, "Scientism,"
Dualism—these have been dominant characteristics of the
Modern Outlook, the Outlook of which we today are, albeit
often unconsciously, the heirs. Every one of these characteristics has profound meaning for the two great interests which
furnish the foci of our theme—*education* and *God*. These
characteristics furnish the larger background for our consideration of the place of religion in American education, to
which we must turn directly in the next chapter.

CHAPTER TWO

THE AMERICAN SCENE

I. The Background.

II. The Foreground.

III. Students Speak.

IV. The British Counterpart.

V. The Present Situation.

CHAPTER TWO
THE AMERICAN SCENE

IN THE preceding chapter, we were occupied with what I have ventured to call the "larger background" of our subject. Very "large," it may have seemed, since it dealt with certain broad trends in the development of Western thought during the Modern Period. And, unduly far "back," since it attempted to discover the origins of our present situation in thinkers of the seventeenth century, notably René Descartes and Immanuel Kant. To be sure, at certain points the outworking of their influence was illustrated in features of American academic thought and life today, but the latter were introduced only by way of illustration.

The time has come when we should bring our attention sharply to focus upon the main theme, "GOD IN EDUCATION." Here, a few words of more limited and concrete historical orientation are essential. We may usefully distinguish three successive epochs with respect to the role of religion in the universities and colleges of the United States; these may be captioned "the Nearer Background," "the Foreground," and "the Present Situation."

I

1. The *Background* of the present American educational scene is the period of its initial beginnings.

As is well known, higher education in the United States

41

was originally almost exclusively under Christian auspices. Colleges were mainly of two types. Earliest were institutions along the Atlantic seaboard, many of which have since developed into "independent," privately endowed universities. Most of them were founded primarily as training schools for the leadership of Government and Church. Representative of them all was the first of them all, Harvard College, the circumstances of whose launching are set forth in these quaint and classic words:

> "After God had carried us safe to *New England,* and wee had builded our houses, provided necessaries for our liveli-hood, rear'd convenient places for Gods worship, and setled the Civill Government: One of the next things we longed for, and looked after was to advance *Learning* and perpetuate it to *Posterity*: dreading to leave an illiterate Ministry to the Churches, when our Ministers shall lie in the Dust. And as wee were thinking and consulting how to effect this great Work; it pleased God to stir up the heart of one Mr. *Harvard* (a godly Gentleman, and a lover of Learning, there living amongst us)." [1]

Sixty-five years later, ten Congregational ministers, all but one of them Harvard graduates, wrote into the charter of Yale College their intention that its students should be so educated that they might be "fitted for publick employment both in Church and Civil state"; four-fifths of the earliest student body at Yale became ministers. Even more explicit and unequivocal was the purpose of King's College, now Columbia University, as set forth by its first president:

> "The chief thing that is aimed at in this college is to teach and engage the children to know God in Jesus Christ, and to love and serve him, in all sobriety, godli-

---

[1] *New England's First Fruits,* quoted in Samuel Eliot Morison, *The Founding of Harvard College,* p. 432.

ness, and righteousness of life, with a perfect heart, and a willing mind; and to train them up in all virtuous habits, and all such useful knowledge as may render them creditable to their families and friends, ornaments to their country and useful to the public weal in their generations."

President Samuel Johnson went on to make clear that, while there was to be no sectarian indoctrination, the college would aim "to inculcate upon their tender minds, the great principles of Christianity and morality, in which true Christians of each denomination are generally agreed." [2] Very similar were the auspices and impulses which started William and Mary, Princeton, Dartmouth, Pennsylvania and the other pioneers.[3] So powerful and persistent was this initial Christian influence that, in not a few of these institutions, their presidents until quite recently have usually been ordained clergymen.

The other type comprised the so-called "Church Colleges"— for the most part, much smaller institutions scattered in every corner of the land, founded by groups of Christians or individual religious Communions primarily in order that the youth of their memberships might have the privilege of the higher learning, to be furnished them in an avowedly and vigorously Christian setting. Most of the institutions of this type still retain some Church connection.

Only in the second period did government-sponsored higher education attain significant proportions.[4] Generally speaking,

[2] *Samuel Johnson, President of King's College, His Career and Writings,* edited by Herbert and Carol Schneider, vol. iv, p. 223.

[3] The historical record has been recently reviewed by President Howard Lowry of Wooster College in *The Mind's Adventure,* Ch. II, from which the above citations are drawn.

[4] Of the 207 colleges established before the Civil War, 180 were denominationally sponsored, 21 were state universities, and 6 were under public or semi-public but not religious auspices. Donald G. Tewksbury, *The Founding of American Colleges and Universities before the Civil War,* p. 90.

until about half a century ago, the relation of religion to collegiate training in America was two-fold. The Church was the parent and sponsor of education. And religion was the keystone of the educational arch, the determining factor in educational theory and practice. This was precisely as most Americans wished. The role of religion in the education of their children exactly mirrored the importance they professed to give it in their own lives. More than that, the role of religion in American higher education in this period of its beginnings closely paralleled the role religion had played with respect to education in the "great tradition," that is, roughly from the birth of Christianity to the dawn of the Modern Period. Throughout that epoch, the Church was prevailingly the guardian of learning and the originator and sponsor of education; and the God of Christian faith was prevailingly recognized as the Ground of Truth and, therefore, the ruling principle of the educational process. The fact that the originating impulses of higher education in America sprang largely as aftermaths of the religious revivals of the eighteenth and early nineteenth centuries and that the Church was their channel served to reproduce on this continent something of the circumstances and presuppositions which had parented the "great tradition" at the very time when that tradition was progressively losing its hold upon education on the continent of its origin. Indeed, in this as in other respects, history in this country has traversed in two centuries the course which in the more leisurely development of the Old World occupied nearly two millennia.

II

2. In the middle period, developments in education continued to reflect those in national life as a whole. For the American people, the past five decades have been years of

rapid and far-reaching change. So, likewise, this *foreground* was marked by striking modifications in the dimensions, the orientation, and the philosophy of higher education in this country. Three features stand forth as determinative—*expansion, specialization, secularization.*

(1) *Expansion*—an unprecedented increase of students, of educational institutions, of subject matters. As recently as 1907, a little more than forty years ago, university and college students in this country totaled only 300,000. Thirty years later, their number had multiplied four-fold; ten years later still, nearly ten-fold. If the recommendations of the President's Commission on Higher Education prevail, enrollments in 1960 will reach 4,600,000.[5] These figures suggest both the dimensions of the expansion and its accelerating tempo.

Such rapid increase in clientele could be cared for only by a mushroom growth and multiplication of institutions, of diverse sizes and types, under a variety of auspices, in every section of the country. As late as 1900 only two institutions boasted an enrollment of as much as 2,000. Today some twenty universities report a student body of over 20,000. Gigantic state and municipal schools, supported by public funds, now harbor more than half of our college youth. Many of these vast and marvelous factories of learning turn out A.B.'s, B.S.'s, M.A.'s, even Ph.D.'s very much like a Ford factory—standard products, brightly resplendent and efficient, as well equipped as a Ford car for the hard work, the wear and tear, of life; and as ill-equipped for adjustment to the varied demands, or mediation of the more delicate aspects, of life.

However, multiplication was not only in *students* and *institutions*, but also in *subject matters*. These were the decades of the most rapid extension and diversification of knowledge in human history. Accommodation in the structure of education

[5] *Higher Education for American Democracy*, I, 49–50.

was inevitable. The larger universities multiplied schools and divisions; in some of them, it is a dull year which does not record the launching of at least one new division. The smaller colleges multiplied departments. All multiplied subjects and courses within almost every department. This development has flourished all along the line, but with most jubilant unrestraint in the so-called "practical" and vocational fields, rather than in the traditional and humanistic disciplines. Not only have the *dimensions* of the typical curriculum swollen almost beyond recognition; the traditional *balance* within the curriculum has altered even more drastically.

(2) With this expansion of subject matter and multiplication of academic divisions and departments has gone a second feature of the period, namely, *specialization*—concentration of attention by both teachers and students upon some one problem, or phase of a problem, to the neglect of its organic connections and its larger setting.

Specialization is one of the most obvious and omnipresent features of our life today. It is a principal curse of *modern industrialization*, in which each workman has responsibility for a smaller and smaller fragment of the total process, less and less awareness of the whole to which he contributes so seemingly insignificant a part. It is a striking characteristic—many believe, a regrettable characteristic—of *modern medicine*, in which each practitioner deals with a single organ or function, few with the organism in its entirety, with the patient in his total being. Of specialization, our academic communities furnish extreme illustration. Specialization in scholarship, and a corresponding narrowing of the area of competence of each scholar. Specialization in study, and a corresponding constriction of the horizons of each student. Specialization—so essential for scientific advance, so productive of increased knowledge. Specialization—so stunting to large-mindedness, so fatal to comprehension of the *whole* truth, that is, the *real* truth. It is this which has prompted the hackneyed student jibe that a university professor is a man who knows more and more about less and less. It has led perhaps the foremost thinker of this country in these latter days, Professor Whitehead of Harvard, to his more considered, more authoritative, and more devastating indictment: "The increasing departmentalization of universities during the last hundred years, however necessary for administrative purposes, tends to trivialize the mentality of the teaching profession." [6] And, one must add, I fear, not only the mentality of those who teach, but, hardly less, by contagion and reflection, the mentality of those who are taught.

The twin features of *multiplication* and *specialization* find their most striking expression in the present-day university curriculum and the assumptions which underlie it. And it is through the curriculum, which under the free elective system is offered for unguided choice, that these factors make their major impact upon the mind of the student. The contemporary university curriculum reminds one of nothing so much as a lavish cafeteria, where unnumbered tasty intellectual delicacies are strung along a moving belt for individual selection without benefit of dietary advice or caloric balance. "The bargain-counter theory of education," Dr. William Adams Brown once called it. I have myself confronted a transcript of record from a respectable state university which testified to the student's competence, as a Bachelor of Arts, to pursue postgraduate training in philosophy and theology by the fact that he had successfully completed courses in Band, Military Science, Folk Dancing, Swimming, Animal Husbandry and Mortuary Science. And the result in the mind of the student? All too often, obesity or mental indigestion; or, it may be, malnutrition and even pernicious intellectual anemia.

[6] A. N. Whitehead, *Nature and Life*, p. 16.

To invoke the name of President Hutchins in any discussion of educational theory or practice is to risk immediate alienation of at least half one's audience; perhaps that is too conservative an estimate of the defection. But one must take that risk in loyalty to complete candor. I should wish to confess my judgment that, in Dr. Hutchins' initial critique of present-day education in *The Higher Learning in America*, whatever one's view of his proposals for cure, his diagnosis of disease was disturbingly accurate. Like many a patient, revulsion from the treatment prescribed has furnished a comfortable excuse for evading the soundness of the physician's analysis of our symptoms. Speaking of the very matters which have just been concerning us—chaos in the curriculum and the anarchy of a free elective system, and their effect upon minds of both faculty and student—he said in part:

"The modern university may be compared with an encyclopedia. The encyclopedia contains many truths. It may consist of nothing else. But its unity can be found only in its alphabetical arrangement. The university is in much the same case. It has departments running from art to zoology; but neither the students nor the professors know what is the relation of one departmental truth to another, or what the relation of departmental truths to those in the domain of another department may be."

"The free elective system as applied to professors means that they can follow their own bents, gratify their own curiosity, and offer courses in the results. The accumulation of credits in these courses must lead, like those in any other courses, to the highest academic degrees. Discrimination among courses would be undemocratic. The student would, then, confront an enormous miscellany, composed principally of current or historical investigations in a terrifying multiplicity of fields."

"The free elective system as Mr. Eliot introduced it at Harvard and as Progressive Education adapted it to lower age levels amounted to a denial that there was content to education. Since there was no content to education, we might as well let students follow their own bent. They would at least be interested and pleased and would be as well educated as if they had pursued a prescribed course of study. This overlooks the fact that the aim of education is to connect man with man, to connect the present with the past, and to advance the thinking of the race. If this is the aim of education, it cannot be left to the sporadic, spontaneous interests of children or even of undergraduates."

"Unless students and professors (and particularly professors) have a common intellectual training, a university must remain a series of disparate schools and departments, united by nothing except the fact that they have the same president and board of trustees. Professors cannot talk to one another, not at least about anything important. They cannot hope to understand one another." [7]

But, to get back from effects to causes, to first principles, the prevailing assumption, plainly testified by the structure of the curriculum and the manner of teaching even when not openly avowed, is that knowledge consists of countless fragments of truth, spread forth higgledy-piggledy, to be savored and swallowed like so many morsels of intellectual pabulum. This stands in radical contrast to the traditional assumption of the organic interrelatedness and unity of truth. But is that the character of truth of which human knowledge is the apprehension? Or is Truth, as the ancient tradition assumed, an organic unity, each several part being what it is by virtue of its place within the whole?

[7] Robert Maynard Hutchins, *The Higher Learning in America* (Yale University Press), pp. 95, 92, 71, 59.

(3) Finally, *multiplication* and *specialization* have been paralleled, as both effect and cause, by progressive *secularization*.

With mercurial enlargement in the dimensions of American higher education have gone kaleidoscopic mutations in educational theory and practice. These were partly a result of the emergence of the Modern Mind of which we said something in the preceding chapter. More important, however, they reflected changes, not primarily in the dominant philosophies, but rather in the ideals and habits of American life. Men always attribute disproportionate influence to intellectual factors, to trends of thought. This error is especially rife in academic communities. Since their main concern is with the intellectual enterprise, they can hardly resist the assumption that their labors are forming the character of the national mind, if not fully moulding policies in national life. They forget that that which determines both individual and corporate outlooks far more than theory is always the actual character of the practical world of affairs which surrounds and moulds both. This is notably true in this land of ours. With us more than with most peoples, action precedes thought; practice dictates principle; what we do determines what we believe.

The new educational philosophy was born of the times. Its presuppositions, norms and objectives mirrored the public mind. It echoed the typical American's glorification of the individual, his disdain of the past, his trust in science as mankind's Messiah, his inveterate optimism, his unchallengeable certitude of the fated prosperity and progress of his own nation, his estimate of the true values of life, his delight in gadgets and techniques, his religious unconcern, above all his unshakable confidence in man's power to know and to do—in brief, his this-worldly perspective. The end-product of this drift in national life is the modern, successful American whom

Struthers Burt once characterized as that "strange, absurd, pathetic conquering Hamlet of the modern world, with his catch words and his motor cars, a score of platitudes on his lips and a score of unrealized desires in his heart." And his feminine counterpart—the modern American woman who, as Walter Lippmann satirizes her, "has emancipated herself from the tyranny of fathers, husbands and homes, and, with the intermittent but expensive help of a psychoanalyst, is now enduring liberty as an interior decorator."

Only in this larger setting can we rightly interpret the progressive secularization of American education. Let us not be deceived as to its causes. While it may be attributed in some small part to the proliferation of knowledge and the resultant increasing complexity of curricular structure, it is mainly an accurate reflection of what has been taking place through the past half century in the life of the American people as a whole. In this progressive secularization of education, we are hard up against the progressive secularization of American life.

As might be expected, the trend has been most powerful in the *state and municipal universities*, partly because, supported by public funds, they are most sensitive and responsive to what the general public desires; partly because many of them, emerging late upon the scene, were anchored to no tradition of the earlier period and faced no vestigial remains of that tradition, to come to terms with or to shake off. As we have pointed out, it is these publicly supported schools which now harbor a full half of the college youth.[8] While the provisions for religious instruction and other religious influences

[8] Of the 1,700 institutions of higher education in the United States at the present time, just under one third are publicly controlled and supported, 27% are privately endowed, and 40% are "church-related." Students are almost equally divided between publicly sponsored institutions and all others, whether privately endowed or church-related. Cp. the pre-Civil War figures above, p. 43, footnote 4.

in state institutions are far more general and more generous than is usually supposed,[9] most of them today have no definite philosophy of the relation of God to truth, therefore of the role of religion within education.

Meanwhile, the older educational institutions were subject to the same controlling persuasions, and were bent only somewhat more slowly and less fully to their insistent pressures. Most of the *privately endowed, "independent" universities* sloughed off every vestige of ecclesiastical control. Not a few of them still maintain a university-sponsored chapel service, often sparsely attended by a few senior faculty members, fewer undergraduates, and a somewhat larger number of academic camp-followers; but these services are not infrequently bathed in an atmosphere of pious reminiscence, dutiful continuations of ceremonies which once had vital meaning, but no longer. Many *"Christian Colleges"* have become increasingly embarrassed and uncomfortable in their traditional Church connections. As we should expect, the new situation is most strikingly disclosed within their curricula. No longer is religion the keystone of the educational arch, but rather one stone among many, and a stone for which no very logical or satisfactory place within the main structure can be discovered.

Thus has something like a revolution in American higher education occurred within a single generation. As fully as in the earlier period, education reflects the dominant convictions and desires of the national mind. It is still true, as it was fifty or a hundred and fifty years ago, that the American people demand in the education of their children a place for religion comparable to that which they intend to give it in their own devotion. Our educational system has lost what had been its principle of coherence and its instrument of cohesion. Is it too much to say that the same thing is true of the national life?

[9] See below, pp. 111ff.

III

And the youth who have been coming up to the colleges? In considerable numbers, they are grandchildren or great-grandchildren of a pioneering ancestry, but children of the masterful monarchs of prosperity. Not a few are the pride of parents who enjoyed but limited education, who have achieved some measure of wealth and comfort but neither learning nor culture, and who now intend to purchase for their sons and daughters privileges which they themselves were denied. These youth are boys and girls bearing in their bodies and minds the solid resources of their pioneer forebears, sensing within their spirits the restless and puzzling energies of youth, finding themselves thrust down in the midst of the bewildering fascination of a great campus, their minds quickened to activity by the scintillating sophistries of clever but often shallow young (or older?) instructors, their emotions stimulated to unruly pitch by the hectic speed of life about them, as well as by the turbulent ferment of life within, and by the incessant allurement of seductive suggestion on every hand. They are intellectual children of the intellectual *nouveau riche*—products of an age which has absorbed contemporary information all out of proportion to its equipment to understand it, to interpret it, to appraise it, and to assimilate it; accurate reflections of a culture which is glittering, impressive, self-confident, but shallowly rooted in foundations and perspectives which could give it depth and truth and significance.

The more thoughtful of these youth are not unaware of their situation, or deceived as to its causes. Let us listen to two student voices from two of our oldest and strongest eastern universities, both men of outstanding ability and campus leadership. One declares:

"We of the younger generation grew up in a 'practical,' 'rational' world. It was so very practical that there was nothing in which it could believe; it was so very rational that it rationalized its way into an unruffled view of its own destruction. . . .

"It might be expected that in acquiring a liberal education, a group of young men might find ideas and ideals to which they could cling with courage and conviction. But such seems not to be the case. Perhaps nowhere is there so much lip service paid to democratic ideals and so little stern devotion to these ideals as in the American colleges. The question forces itself upon us: What are we here for and what is a liberal education striving toward?"

The other student offers an analysis so closely wrought that spotty quotation and condensation emasculate its argument. After reminding the older generation of the framework of *their* upbringing—traditional Christianity and democracy, eternal principles of right and wrong, the existence of the human soul, a personal God and life after death—the writer poses the question: "But what about us, the youth of America? What have we been taught to revere? When *our elders* refer to eternal verities, absolutist ethics, *we* are likely to recall the lesson your instructors in sociology have driven home—that morals are relative to time and place, that what is good in one society is bad in another. . . . Have we not gleaned from your professors of natural science, philosophy and ancient history that religions are the product of myth and superstition and that men create gods in their own image? . . . Biology now conceives of man as one species of mammal. . . . Free will is at odds with the basic assumption of modern science—determinism. . . . Little of the learning we absorb includes value judgments." Then follow his queries, direct implications of the university's teaching: "If men are but animals, why not treat them as such? If man is a slave to determinism, incapable of free choice, what is the value of the ballot, trial by jury and civil liberties in general? . . . Personally I fail to understand how you can expect us to become ardent Christians and democrats when the vital postulates on which these faiths are supposed to rest are daily undermined in the classroom. . . . Isn't it palpably obvious that the root of the trouble lies in an apparent contradiction between the implications of our studies and the ideals we are expected to revere? Of course we are apathetic, discontent, reluctant to assume the responsibility of thinking and acting. Of course we live solely in the present, without visions of the future, without any firm convictions, hiding under a mask of conventional behavior the 'futilitarianism' the more thoughtful of us clearly recognize, the less thoughtful profoundly sense. . . . We, the young, are the American tragedy."

IV

Thus far in this chapter, we have confined our attention to the American scene. In part, that is because here we are on home territory; we know at first hand its every contour and are in a position to judge whether it is being accurately surveyed and reported. But, also, because here is the sphere of our specific responsibility; if our thought is to lead to action, it must be action directed to American higher education.

But the situation as we have analyzed it is not a distinctively American phenomenon posing an exclusively American problem. On the contrary, a closely parallel account might be given of the recent history of educational trends throughout the Western World, and, more particularly, in that country of our cultural parentage to which we acknowledge both the largest indebtedness for the past and the nearest kinship in the present, Great Britain.

There has recently come from that land by all odds the

most thorough and incisive critique of higher education which
has been formulated in our day. It reports the conclusions of
an unusually able and influential group of British educators.
It has been penned by a man who is qualified by wider and
more intimate acquaintance with the length and breadth of
higher education throughout Great Britain than probably any
other individual. Sir Walter Moberley is a graduate of New
College, Oxford, a distinguished philosopher, and former Vice-
chancellor of the University of Manchester. Through the last
fifteen years he has served as Chairman of the University
Grants Committee, the body charged with allocating the vast
funds which the British Government contributes in support
of its universities and colleges. The title of his book is *The
Crisis in the University*. Many regard it as the most important
work on education written in this century.

That we may see our American issues in the larger context
of the English-speaking world, let me put before you some
of its representative statements: [10]

> "Beneath the façade of development and hopefulness,
> the British universities today share with the universities
> of the world a peculiar malaise and impotence. They have
> little inner self-confidence, because they lack, and are in-
> creasingly aware that they lack, any clear, agreed sense
> of direction and purpose. . . .
>
> "The most cogent evidence of this 'sickness' is the gulf
> between appearance and reality, between the ideals to
> which the university traditionally professes allegiance, and
> for which it mostly still supposes itself to stand, and the
> springs of action by which it is really moved. . . .
>
> "Whatever the cause, the university today lives and
> moves and has its being in a moral and cultural fog. . . .

[10] The positions Sir Walter Moberley develops are so closely analogous to
the argument I have attempted to present that perhaps I should say that
these pages were completed before his volume came into my hands. What he
has written has confirmed not formed my own thinking.

"The effect of this tendency is narrowness in the individual and fragmentation in the university. In the words of Archbishop William Temple, a university becomes 'a place where a multitude of studies are conducted, with no relation between them except those of simultaneity and juxtaposition.' " (pp. 21, 23, 28, 58--59)

Searching for the underlying causes of the current malaise, Sir Walter finds them in these facts:

"The university today is not asking the really fundamental questions. . . .

"We have a semi-instinctive disposition to shy away sharply like a nervous horse from any question arousing strong emotion or likely to involve commitment at a deep level. This has its creditable side. . . . But a praiseworthy reticence in the expression of one's innermost convictions is one thing; to have no such convictions to express is another. . . .

"On practical affairs the academic mind is prone to reach a state of permanently suspended judgment, of conscientious indecision. . . . Many a scholar spends his life in accumulating data for some *magnum opus* which he never writes; or, if he does write it, his book consists of prolegomena." (pp. 50, 51, 53–54)

Speaking of the outworking of this situation within the universities upon their students, Sir Walter concludes:

"For the majority of students. . . , their university has been less an *Alma Mater* than a bargain-counter, at which certain specific articles they require are purveyed. . . .

"Our young men do not see visions, but they dream troubled dreams. . . .

"The best of our young men are disillusioned, suspicious of idealistic appeals as 'baited by knaves to set a trap for fools,' disinclined to accept any moral code at second hand or from convention. . . .

"Mentally and spiritually, most persons today are 'displaced persons'. . . .

"Our predicament then is this. Most students go through our universities without ever having been forced to exercise their minds on the issues which are really momentous. Under the guise of academic neutrality they are subtly conditioned to unthinking acquiescence in the social and political *status quo* and in a secularism on which they have never seriously reflected. Owing to the prevailing fragmentation of studies, they are not challenged to decide responsibly on a life-purpose or equipped to make such a decision wisely. They are not incited to disentangle and examine critically the assumptions and emotional attitudes underlying the particular studies they pursue, the profession for which they are preparing, the ethical judgments they are accustomed to make, and the political or religious convictions they hold. Fundamentally they are uneducated." (pp. 24, 18, 57, 16, 70) [11]

V

3. This brings us to the *present situation*. In the past few years, something which may fairly be characterized as a second revolution has quietly been taking its rise in the underlying philosophy of higher education in the United States.

It was foreshadowed by desperate and almost frantic measures advocated, in the years immediately before World War II, in three of our foremost universities. They shared a common aim—to overtake the fatal inadequacies we have suggested. Behind at least two of these three proposals for radical

[11] *The Crisis in the University*. Copyright by The Macmillan Company and used with their permission.

innovations pressed insistent *student* agitation, welling up from profound undergraduate unrest over the jumbled and meaningless chaos of the modern curriculum.

One proposal, by a Yale man at the University of Chicago, was to superimpose upon the entire curriculum the strait jacket of a rehabilitated medieval synthesis. A second was the introduction at Harvard of "roving professors," omniscient purveyors of learning, moving from one field of knowledge to another and vaulting the chasms and barricades which separate their respective custodians, as though in this fashion the university could suggest the unity of truth which the specialized teaching in its various divisions so largely denies. The third, at Princeton, was the inauguration, largely on the initiative of younger instructors in the several departments of the Humanities, of a new Department of Religious Thought, to set forth the Christian tradition as the common foundation of western history, art, literature and philosophy, and therefore the only appropriate principle of integration for the educational process.

These were anticipations of a movement which has advanced on both a wider and deeper front under the solemnizing impetus of wartime self-examination.

Just five years ago, the University of California in Los Angeles circularized forty-seven colleges and universities to discover whether they were contemplating curricular revisions in the postwar period, and if so, what direction those revisions would take. The study embraced institutions representative of every area and type—east, south, central and west; large and small; state-supported and privately endowed. In every case, the institution questioned is recognized as a leader of its area and type. To forty-seven inquiries, forty-one replies were received. Thirty-nine reported committees at work on fundamental curricular change. Thirty indicated plans sufficiently developed to warrant direct answers. The three most important questions inquired whether the institution had made, would make, or was contemplating, changes at the following points:

> Increased emphasis on general education, with decreased opportunity for specialization.
>
> Increased requirement of specific courses or subjects, with decreased privilege of free election.
>
> Increased insistence on distribution of the student's program of study among all the major areas of human knowledge.

Among the thirty institutions which could give definite answers, *affirmative replies to these three questions ran from 75 to 88 per cent.*

Thus is revealed a trend which is nation-wide, which characterizes colleges of every size and type, and which is nearly universal—a trend away from relatively free election toward a fairly large prescription of areas of study if not of specific courses, away from encouragement to specialization toward insistence upon thorough grounding in all the chief fields of human learning. This trend is the direct reversal of the drift which has controlled higher education in America for more than half a century. I have spoken of these changes as a second revolution. They might properly be described as a conversion—an about-face, and an about-face in the right direction.[12]

The major purpose behind all of these new schemes is to introduce larger unity, coherence and therefore meaning, into the undergraduate's course of study. Beneath the proposals lie two assumptions. Both are fundamentally religious assumptions. One concerns the *nature of man*; the other concerns the *nature of truth*.

[12] Another evidence of the same trend is the greatly increased attention during the past few years to the teaching of religion in the universities, to which we shall return below, pp. 73-77, 112-113.

It is assumed that the youth of seventeen to twenty years of age is not competent to decide the essentials of his own education. The college must undertake responsibility to determine, in considerable measure, his choices. And in an age lacking coherence and in a culture crying for cohesion but under the sway of specialized interests and fragmentary loyalties, it must introduce him to the great disciplines of learning which together constitute the foundations of an educated mind.

We are being led back behind a conception which has largely dominated the recent epoch—that man is primarily an intellect to be instructed and informed—to the conception which guided our forebears who first planted schools on this continent, and which led them so prevailingly to place higher education firmly under religious auspices—that human nature is bipolar, mind and soul, and that the concern of learning is with the whole man as with the Whole Truth, to lead forth his mind into an apprehension of that Truth and his soul into a disciplined and obedient loyalty to its imperious commands. The task of education is both to fill the mind and to form the soul.

But the other, and more important, assumption concerns *the nature of truth.* It is, quite simply, the organic unity of all truth, each several part being what it is by virtue of its place within the Whole; and, therefore, the coherence of knowledge which is man's apprehension of truth. But, if truth *is* an organic whole, how does it come to be so? Whence springs its interrelatedness and coherence? What do these imply regarding the nature of Reality? We are driven hard up against the question of God.

To this question, we shall turn in the next chapter.

PROSPECT: WHICH WAY AHEAD?

CHAPTER III

PROSPECT: WHICH WAY AHEAD?

W E BEGAN our inquiry into the relation of God to
education by an analysis of what is spoken of famil-
iarly though often vaguely as the "Modern Mind" or the
"Modern Outlook." We defined its major characteristics as
Individualism, Intellectualism, Modernism, what we have
termed *"Scientism,"* and *Dualism.* Looking backward, we
found the origin of these characteristics in presuppositions and
habits of thought traceable to the early formative thinkers of
the Modern Period, especially René Descartes and Immanuel
Kant. But we also discovered these characteristics in typical
and often extreme expression in contemporary American education. And we noted that each of these characteristics sev-
erally, and all of them together, tend against the acknowledgment of a Living God.

In the preceding chapter, we followed the outworking of
these characteristic features of the Modern Outlook more specifically within the American educational scene during the
recent period of rapid change, of accelerating multiplication,
specialization and secularization. We noted the end-product in
the typical American university of today, in which God has
been largely banished as a consciously recognized factor in
educational philosophy, and religion struggles to maintain a
precarious foothold within the educational structure as a secondary or peripheral adjunct—often a modest and ill-favored

sideshow alongside the main tent. Finally, we made mention of certain marked though inchoate counter-tendencies of very recent origin, reaching out somewhat vaguely for a recovery of religious influences and possibly theistic presuppositions.

What of the way ahead? What *should be* the place of God in education, the role of religion in the educational process?

II

We shall attempt direct and quite specific answers to these questions. But first we must deal briefly with three considerations which were almost wholly overlooked in our historical account. Many would regard these considerations as the principal causative factors in the displacement of religion from its original central position in American higher education to its present secondary or peripheral status, and, even more, as decisive barriers to a restoration of religion to its traditional centrality.

1. The first is the inherent *duality of religion*—the obvious, and highly important, fact that religion always appears in discussions of education, as it does in the life of the community which education seeks to serve, in not one but two connections.

It appears, as we are mainly concerned to consider it in these pages, as claimant to the role of *determinative principle in the educational process as a whole,* affecting vitally and decisively the over-all philosophy and content of the curriculum and of its every part, reflecting religion's basic premise that God is the ultimate Ground of Truth in relation to which every segment of knowledge and all particular truths must be oriented. This claim is simply the counterpart in the realm of learning of the wider contention that religion, since it deals with basic issues and Ultimate Reality, should permeate and direct the whole of life.

But religion appears, also, as *a quite specific interest* distinguishable from the other major interests of the human spirit—art, literature, science, industry, business, sport, etc.; witness the role of the churches in the life of any community. As such, it has a history and a subject matter of its own and therefore claims a place within the enterprise of learning alongside the other principal academic disciplines.

This duality may be recognized as the distinction between *religion* and *the several Religions*. "In which of these two contexts," the religionist may be asked, "do you seek for a recognition of God in education? More specifically, in which sense do you wish religion to find a place within the university curriculum?" The answer is, "Not either-or but both-and." At first hearing, however, that sounds like an extravagant and unreasonable demand. The academic community, always somewhat jealously minded, is disposed to rejoin, "You religionists cannot have it both ways. Make up your minds whether you intend to interpret religion as, properly, the controlling factor in all life and therefore the governing principle of all knowledge; in which case give up the attempt to insert religion as a special subject with its own department in the curriculum. Or, alternatively, recognize the realities of the situation—that religion is, in fact, one among the multifarious and diverse interests of mankind, deserving of such place as it can win as a subject for special study, in which case surrender this vaulting contention that religion should penetrate and guide the whole curriculum, indeed, the entire university program." The admonition is usually implied if not explicit that the religionists would be well advised to limit their efforts to the second alternative.

With respect to this duality, it is quite clear what has actually happened in the history of American education. As we noted above, in the earliest days religion was recognized as "the keystone of the educational arch, the determining factor in educational theory and practice," though the history and beliefs of Christianity also appeared as one subject, an indispensable subject, often a required subject, in the student's plan of study. In the past half-century, religion has been almost universally displaced from its unique role as keystone; at the most, a department of religion has been retained, or recently reinstated, as one among the ever-multiplying disciplines of a full-orbed academic calendar—as we have suggested, "one stone among many, and a stone for which no very logical or satisfactory place within the main structure can be discovered." Note that this alteration and reduction of status is closely analogous to the outcome, in the wider arena of Modern Thought, of the false and unhappy Cartesian and Kantian dualisms, to which we pointed in Chapter One. Sir Walter Moberley well describes the present situation in Great Britain:

> "Lately any corporate action of Christians in university affairs has tended to be sectional. It has been concerned with retaining or winning a small 'place in the sun' for specifically 'religious' interests. Thus Christians have striven to make good a claim for the creation of a Faculty of Theology or for the inclusion of some form of religious teaching among the options for a general degree, or to set up here and there a Hall of Residence under religious auspices as a small enclave in the middle of a secular university. Certainly such things have their value. But the main question which concerns us is quite different. It is this: 'What can Christian insight contribute to enable the university *to be the university?'* " [1]

Translate two or three of the British terms into their American equivalents, and do we not have a surprisingly accurate description of our own situation?

[1] Walter Moberley, *The Crisis in the University*, p. 26. Copyright by The Macmillan Company and used with their permission.

2. The second complication arises from the *plurality of Religions*, a fact confronting education in almost every land, and nowhere more strikingly or confusingly than in this land of ours.

"Religion in education! *Which* Religion?" it may be asked. "So long as the populace of this country was predominantly Christian and even Protestant, that was a practicable, even if questionable, proposal. But today—with the population sharply divided in allegiance between three major faiths, and no-faith, and Protestants further divided into more than 250 sects—how *could* education make religion its governing principle?"

Note that this difficulty should pertain only to religion in the second of its two meanings—not religion but *the* Religions. It *does* complicate the problem of a department of religion in the curriculum; it poses the dilemma of how to provide exposition of a specific Religion for a student body which adheres to a variety of Religions or none at all. On the other hand, in their conception of the religious orientation of all knowledge, of the place of God in education as a whole, the three major faiths of the Western world—Judaism, Roman Catholicism and Protestantism—hold closely analogous if not identical views, for the good and sufficient reason that their conceptions of God and of His relation to Truth stem from the same source.

3. The third complication is peculiar to the American scene. It is our traditional national dogma of the *"separation of Church and State."* In its bearing upon education, especially public education, this is a special instance of the wider problem of plurality of religious allegiances.

At the present hour, this cherished American principle is being refurbished and redefined to ends for which it was never intended. The Constitutional guarantees of "freedom of religion" have lately been reinterpreted by no less august a body than the United States Supreme Court with meanings which were never foreseen by, and which, it may safely be suggested, would have outraged, the framers of the Constitution. As we all know, the Founding Fathers, however loose some of them may have sat to particular religious dogmas of their day, were, almost without exception, profoundly and convincedly religious men, sincere believers in God, as their frequent references to Him and man's dependence upon Him throughout the founding documents abundantly attest. We do not associate the name of Benjamin Franklin with orthodox belief or even notable piety; but he once summarized a lifetime's reflection as follows:

> "I have lived, sir, a long time. And the longer I live, the more convincing proofs I see of this truth—that God governs in the affairs of men. And if a sparrow cannot fall to the ground without His notice, is it probable that an empire can rise without His aid? We have been assured, sir, in the sacred writings that except the Lord build the house, they labor in vain that build it. I firmly believe this; and I also believe that without His concurring aid we shall succeed in this political building no better than the builders of Babel; our projects will be confounded and we ourselves shall become a reproach and a byword down to future ages." [2]

A nation without religious faith, or a system of education for that nation's youth without implicit, and probably explicit, recognition of God as the ground of Truth, would doubtless have stirred the authors of the Constitution to profounder misgivings regarding the future of the country they were seeking to create than the menace of the most powerful foes

---

[2] Closely parallel declarations by almost all of the Founding Fathers could be cited. See the fuller discussion of these issues below, pp. 102–108.

abroad or the most treacherous tyranny at home. It has been aptly said: they were seeking to provide freedom *of* religion, not freedom *from* religion. They intended to exclude, not faith but sectarianism.

In any event, as we just remarked in commenting upon the broader problem created by a plurality of Religions wherever found, the principle of "separation of Church and State" may complicate the question of the content of teaching in a department of religion within a university; it hardly touches the larger issue which is our main concern—the fundamental orientation of the entire institution and its total course of study. The failure of the three major faiths and of the uncounted Protestant denominations to discern this fact and to join forces in a united philosophy of religiously-oriented learning and a united program to preserve this character to American higher education has undoubtedly been a contributing factor in the progressive secularization of education in this country. To that degree, sectarianism bears responsibility for the very outcome it decries. Especially with respect to the public schools, it is blameworthy not only for surrendering them to a strictly secular philosophy of education, but also and more serious, for betraying what should be the basic and invulnerable conviction of *all* faiths alike—that teaching which does not recognize God as the ultimate Ground of Truth is false teaching.

III

An adequate consideration of the total question of religion in education would require equal treatment of the two aspects of the matter—the significance of God for the philosophy and structure of education as a whole, and the place and specific content of the teaching of religion within the curriculum. It is the latter question which has received major emphasis in recent discussions. It is the latter which is presently to the fore in public attention, drawn there by the current disputes over the appropriateness of religious instruction in educational institutions, whether publicly or privately supported, especially the public schools. I have no doubt that it was the latter of these two aspects of the matter which sprang most readily to the reader's mind in response to the title of this book. Doubtless it was expected that much would be said about religious departments or courses in the curriculum, college chapel whether required or optional, the role of student-sponsored religious societies such as Christian Associations, the cultivation of religious sympathies and loyalties among faculty members as individuals, etc., etc.

These are large and important matters. If we touch upon them briefly, it is mainly lest consideration of them deflect attention from the more fundamental and important issue.

Suffice it to point out that the fact of *plurality of Religions* in American culture has not prevented the development of sound and strong religious instruction in institutions of each type—Church Colleges, privately endowed universities, and state-supported schools.

The *Church Colleges should* confront no difficulty in principle, though some of them have, in fact, been very uncomfortable in their present practices. Founded under Christian sponsorship for the explicit purpose of providing higher education in a Christian setting, they are obviously free to establish for their educational enterprise such Christian terms of reference as they may deem right; or, perhaps more accurately, as their present Boards of Trustees, with a practical eye toward student enrollments and student fees, are prepared to maintain. The problem, here, is not one of law or of right; it is a problem of conviction and courage.[3]

[3] On the position and problems of the Church College, see the admirable discussion in Howard Lowry, *The Mind's Adventure*, Ch. IV: "Liberal Education and Religion: The Church College."

The *privately supported universities* do not find themselves in essentially different circumstance. Their independence of public funds enables and entitles them to determine both the philosophy and the content of their curricula. No student is required to take advantage of their offerings. None is justified, nor are his parents, in challenging the institution's right to determine its own program. In most instances, moreover, what is at stake is merely the content, in a department of religion, of courses which are offered students for free choice or rejection. As a matter of fact, many of the strongest institutions in the land—to name just a few on the Atlantic seaboard, Harvard, Yale, Princeton, Williams, Amherst, Wellesley, Vassar, Smith—have for years offered courses in religion on a full parity both as to scholarly excellence and as to academic recognition with the teaching in science, history, philosophy or literature, and such courses are highly regarded and widely elected by successive generations of students. One of the most interesting straws in the present-day wind is the marked increases in enrollment which these courses have enjoyed in recent years and the consequent expansion of the faculties in the religious field.[4] Even more significant is the inauguration within the past five years of *new* departments of religion along similar lines, notably at the University of Pennsylvania and Columbia University, and the intention of New York University and Leland Stanford shortly to follow suit. The presuppositions justifying and guiding such teaching may be summarized as follows: Religion is a perennial, ineradicable and vital concern of the human spirit. Moreover, religion has been and continues to be one of the most formative influences upon every aspect of human culture. Acquaintance with its history, its literature and its teachings is a *sine qua non* for the edu-

[4] For summaries of the factual evidence, see Clarence P. Shedd, "The Agencies of Religion in Higher Education," *Religious Education*, XXXVIII, 5, pp. 290–294; and Merrimon Cuninggim, *The College Seeks Religion*, Ch. X.

cated man or woman. In Western Civilization in general and in American culture in particular, Christianity has been and is the predominant Religion. To that faith, the sponsors of this university acknowledge allegiance, as do the overwhelming majority of those who seek education under its guidance. Therefore, the institution is entitled, indeed obligated, to offer its students the best possible instruction in the history, Scriptures and beliefs of Christianity. Very often, however, teaching in the companion faith of Judaism is also provided, and not infrequently in comparative religion.[5]

The problem for *publicly supported institutions* is, admittedly, more difficult. But that it is far from insoluble is proven conclusively by the sheer facts of present practices in state universities. In the last normal pre-War year, 1941, of 70 state institutions accredited by the Association of American Universities, 21 or 30% actually had full-fledged departments of religion, while 35 more offered courses in religion in other departments of the university, and 6 others gave academic credit for work in religion done in schools or colleges located near the university but not supported by it. Thus students in 62 of the 70 state schools, or almost 90%, had opportunity for academically recognized instruction in religion.[6] According to Professor Clarence P. Shedd, our leading authority in this matter, "At least a dozen state colleges and universities have established chairs or departments of religion, officially sponsored and financed, since the last War."

Either of two alternative points of view may guide the state institution in the development of its program of religious instruction. On the one hand, it may be recognized that re-

[5] Brief descriptions of "Significant Programs" in half a dozen "Independent Colleges" are given in Cuninggim, *op. cit.,* pp. 183ff.

[6] Cuninggim, *op. cit.,* pp. 147, 293–306. The present practice of state institutions in offering religious instruction is discussed more fully below, pp. 111ff.

ligion is a vital and well-nigh universal phenomenon in human life, and that beneath and behind the several specific faiths, certainly those which are found in any strength among Americans, there lie a common body of beliefs and closely parallel experiences and aspirations. It is this "common core" which the teaching of the university should mainly seek to set forth. The presuppositions of such a "common core" have been spelled out by a group of distinguished American educators who are editing a series of brochures on "Religious Perspectives of College Teaching":

> "Religion is man's quest for communion with an ultimate spiritual reality completely independent of human desires and imaginings. Religion apprehends this Absolute Reality and Value in faith, and seeks to give concrete embodiment to the ineffable in creed, cult, and conduct. The creative power of the universe is not an intellectual abstraction but an objective entity, a Divine Being. Although God infinitely transcends our human nature and understanding, He most potently reveals Himself to those who conceive of Him in personal terms. Thus symbolized, He becomes for us not merely Cosmic Mind, but Creator, Judge and Redeemer of mankind." [7]

Such a philosophy has recently been advocated by the International Council of Religious Education:

> "Faith in God, the God of the Old and New Testaments, and faith in free men as His responsible creations have inspired our life and history from the early days of the nation and in its earlier Colonial history. This faith is embodied in our laws, documents, and institutions.

[7] "Religious Perspectives of College Teaching." Edward W. Hazen Foundation. (For full list of titles, cf. Bibliography, pp. 119ff. below.) See also, *College Reading and Religion*, A Survey of College Reading Materials, sponsored by the Edward W. Hazen Foundation and the Committee on Religion and Education of the American Council on Education.

. . . As far as the school can, in view of the religious diversity of our people, judicial opinions, and our American tradition, we expect it to teach this common religious tradition as the only adequate basis for the life of the school and the personal lives of teachers, students, and citizens in a free and responsible democracy." [8]

This is very similar to the principle which has guided Great Britain in the development of her very remarkable new scheme of universal teaching of religion in the publicly sponsored schools under the Education Act of 1944.

Alternatively, the state institution may make its start from the very plurality of Religions in American culture, which is often advanced as an insurmountable barrier to religious instruction in public schools and colleges. Granted the basic recognition that the public to which the institution is responsible holds allegiance in varying degrees to three great faiths—Judaism, Roman Catholicism and Protestantism—and the provision that the history and teachings of all three faiths shall find place in its curriculum, it appears reasonable that state institutions might well model their departments of religion closely upon the best experience of the private universities. Three conditions appear essential—that the teaching should meet the standards of objectivity and scholarly competence expected of every other discipline and not be an instrument

[8] International Council of Religious Education, "Report of the Committee on Religion and Public Education," p. 5. This point of view is strongly espoused by Dr. Ordway Tead, "A Layman's View of the Place of Religion in Public Education," in *Religion and Public Education*, American Council on Education Studies, Series I, No. 22, Vol. ix, February 1945, pp. 33ff. The "common core" principle is vigorously criticized by the Committee on Religion and Education of the American Council on Education, *The Relation of Religion to Public Education*, American Council on Education, 1947; and by Dr. F. Ernest Johnson, "The Role of Religion in General Education," *Teachers College Record*, Vol. 51, No. 4, January 1950, pp. 222ff. But Dr. Johnson explains, "What we object to is the indoctrination of specific religious beliefs in tax-supported institutions."

of sectarian propaganda, that the major religious traditions should be appropriately represented, and that no student should be *required* to come under instruction hostile to his or her parents' convictions. If those conditions are adequately and conscientiously met, there seems no good reason why objection should be raised, by students, by parents or by the general public, or why the Courts should discover, in either the letter or the intent of the national Constitution or most state Constitutions, grounds for proscription. Just such teaching with full academic credit has been offered for years in a number of state universities, sometimes with expenses met wholly through the institution's own funds, sometimes, as at the University of Missouri and Michigan State, with costs defrayed from funds outside the regular university budget. Recently, a full-fledged department of religion set up on these principles was inaugurated at the University of North Carolina, supported by an endowment specifically earmarked for that purpose and by other state funds; at least one other of the foremost state universities is even now planning to follow its example.

The problem of religious instruction at the *high school and grammar school* levels is more complex, and very much more controversial. However, the conviction may be offered that, granted the soundness of the same premises and the fulfillment of the same conditions, there is nothing in principle which should invalidate a closely parallel policy and procedure on either of the two alternative bases outlined above, or on a combination of the two bases. The success of Great Britain in developing "agreed syllabi" for the teaching of religion in all publicly supported schools, with the full concurrence and support of the three major faiths, supplies the proof. It should challenge American educators to fresh efforts to restore religion to its appropriate place within our school curricula.

IV

However, our major concern is not with detailed problems of specifically religious instruction in schools and colleges, but with the larger issues of the orientation of the over-all philosophy of education. These *are* the main issues both because they are more fundamental and because they force us to come to grips with education's avowed central concern and regnant loyalty—the question of truth.

In the last chapter, we referred to widespread re-examination of fundamental educational philosophy among the universities and colleges of the nation, prompted by, and carried forward within, the sobering atmosphere of wartime self-scrutiny. We noted that the great majority of institutions reported that they were preparing to institute radical curricular reform. And that these reforms, prevailingly, contemplated increased emphasis on general education with decreased opportunity for specialization, increased requirement of specific courses or subjects with decreased privilege of free election, increased insistence on distribution of the student's program of study among all the major areas of human knowledge. In sum, they embody a trend away from relatively free elections toward a fairly large prescription of areas of study if not of specific courses, and away from encouragement of specialization toward an insistence upon thorough grounding in all the chief fields of learning, a trend which represents a direct reversal of the drift which has dominated higher education in America for more than half a century. We pointed out that, behind all of these proposals, whatever their contrasts in detail, lie *two assumptions*, and that both are fundamentally religious assumptions—an assumption concerning the *nature of man* and, more particularly, the limited competence of young men and women to determine the essentials of their own education; and an assumption concerning the *nature of truth*. It is to this latter assumption that we now turn. And here we come directly to what I conceive to be the nub of the matter, and the single, central contention of this book.

We may take illustrations from the three ancient universities of the Atlantic seaboard which are so often linked—Harvard, Yale and Princeton. Their plans appear to be furthest advanced, and have already been put into operation. Among reforms thus announced, theirs are perhaps the most noteworthy. Moreover, the prestige of these leaders justifies special attention to their decisions. But the closely parallel proposals of the "Big Three" are important less because of any influence they may exert upon others than as symptomatic of a tidal movement now in full flow. The Harvard Report on *General Education in a Free Society* voices grave concern over the prevailing chaos in American culture; it points to the "supreme need of American education for a unifying purpose and idea"; it proposes to overtake the present lack by introducing each undergraduate to "a common body of information and ideas which would be in some measure the possession of all students."[9] Thus Harvard's motivation is primarily pragmatic, expediential—to further unity in American society by grounding leaders in a common subject matter. Yale and Princeton take higher ground. They face squarely the ultimate issue of the unity of truth, and therefore of the coherence of knowledge which is man's apprehension of truth. The Yale Report affirms that "knowledge for all its convenient compartmentalization is essentially one piece, as is the life which supports that knowledge.[10] And the Princeton Plan takes as its guiding principle the "two-fold belief in the unity of knowledge and the diversity of human beings." [11]

[9] Pp. 43, 191–192.
[10] *Report of the Committee on the Course of Study (Adopted by Faculty, Spring 1945)*, p. 8.
[11] *Plan of Study Leading to the Degree of Bachelor of Arts*, p. 1.

The organic unity of truth, each several part being what it is by virtue of its place within the Whole; and, therefore, *the coherence of knowledge* which is man's apprehension of truth. This is the presupposition which underlies when it does not explicitly determine the reorganization of curricula. But, as we inquired at the close of the last chapter, if truth *is* an organic whole, how does it come to be so? Whence derives its interrelatedness and coherence? What do these imply regarding the nature of Reality? Obviously we are being compelled to consider the most basic of all issues for education. More specifically, we are being driven hard up against the question of God.

To be sure, no human mind, or all together, ever succeeds in encompassing that Whole. But, by the same token, no human mind rightly grasps any fragment of truth without at least some dim awareness of the Whole which gives the fragment its existence and its meaning. Moreover, if Truth be an organism, then every subject and every principal subdivision should be so presented as to suggest that unity. Any segment of knowledge which is portrayed without recognition of its organic relatedness to all other knowledge is being falsely presented. It is not Truth which is being set forth. And, need it be argued, that is unsound education, a betrayal of education's primary and regnant loyalty. As Newman once declared, God has "relations of His own towards the subject-matter of each particular science which the book of knowledge unfolds." [12] One of Newman's early colleagues boldly spelled out the implications of this basic principle:

> "All things must speak of God, refer to God, or they are atheistic. History, without God, is a chaos without design or end or aim. Political economy, without God, would be a selfish teaching about the acquisition of

[12] John Henry Newman, *On the Scope and Nature of University Education,* p. 27.

wealth, making the larger portion of mankind animate machines for its production; Physics, without God, would be a dull enquiry into certain meaningless phenomena; Ethics, without God, would be a varying rule without principle, or substance, or center, or ruling hand; Metaphysics, without God, would make man his own temporary god, to be resolved, after his brief hour here, into the nothingness out of which he proceeded. All sciences . . . will tend to exclude the thought of God if they are not cultivated with reference to Him. History will become an account of man's passions and brute strength, instead of the ordering of God's providence for His creatures' good; Physics will materialize man, and Metaphysics God." [13]

Obviously, this point cuts very deep indeed. What it implies is not merely the institution of courses in religion as one department in the curriculum, or required attendance on such courses. Or a more sympathetic attitude toward one or another of the specific Religions or religion in general on the part of individual faculty members in their private capacities. What it demands is a fundamental reorientation of *every* subject in the curriculum and its presentation in every course.

Do not conjure up the bugaboo of an extreme application of this principle. It is not proposed that every lecture room should be transformed into a church, and each teacher into a preacher. Nor is it suggested for one moment that scholars should be expected to give an interpretation of their subjects which they do not sincerely accept as matters of their own conviction. What *is* most earnestly urged is that, *if* the basic premise is sound—that Truth is an organic unity and each segment of knowledge what it is by virtue of its place within that unity—then no part of knowledge, whatever its subject matter, will be truly and rightly taught unless that relationship

[13] Edward B. Pusey, *Collegiate and Professional Teaching and Discipline*, p. 25. Quoted in Moberley, *op. cit.*, p. 265.

to the Unity of Truth is assumed and, so far as is appropriate, pointed out. And, further, that the educational institution itself which is responsible for the total setting-forth of the *whole* Truth should consciously recognize the basic premise of its undertaking and its responsibility, and acknowledge the Divine Mind without which its enterprise could not take place.

A group of college professors, facing what would be expected of them as teachers if they were to carry out their institution's determination to replace exclusively specialized courses by courses in general education, protested that they would have to go back to graduate school and take their doctorates all over again. To which a somewhat harsh but not inapt rejoinder might have been, perhaps that is exactly what they should do. In the same fashion, instructors confronted with the major contention just advanced might protest that, if they were adequately to teach their several subjects in conformity to the basic premise of the Unity of Truth, they would be compelled to recast the underlying structure of their minds. To which it might be replied, perhaps that is just what is required, *if* they are to fulfill their central loyalty to Truth.

There is a further implication. By the same token, religion, that is, a true knowledge of God, far from being a peripheral or incidental subject in the scheme of education—one stone located here or there haphazard in the educational arch—*is* the Queen of the Sciences, "the architectonic science whose office it is to receive the results of all other sciences and to combine them in an organic whole." [14] This is its rightful position, not because the Churches say so, or because superstition or tradition has so imposed it upon human credulity, or because it was so recognized in one great age of learning, but *because of the nature of Reality*—because, if there be a God at all, He must be the ultimate and controlling Reality

[14] Hastings Rashdall, *The Universities of Europe in the Middle Ages*, Vol. III, p. 442.

through which all else derives its being; and the truth concerning Him, as man can best apprehend it, must be the keystone of the ever-incomplete arch of human knowledge. Learning which does not confess Him as its Foundation because the Determiner of the conditions which render its enterprise possible, and which does not aspire to Him as its Goal, is false learning, however impressive its achievements and pretentious its claims.[15]

For many years past, those who have sought to mediate religious faith to college youth have felt themselves up against almost insuperable obstacles in the very premises of the educational system. In the end of the day, the gravest secularization of American education has not been in the gradual elimination of religious instruction or required chapel, or even in the irreligious outlook of faculties. It has been the secularization of educational theory and structure. Their covert assumptions concerning the two basic factors with which they have to deal—truth and man—have been non-religious. And they have been false. As Sir Walter Moberley well argues:

> "On the fundamental religious issue [the existence of God], the modern university intends to be, and supposes it is, neutral, but it is not. Certainly it neither inculcates nor expressly repudiates belief in God. But it does what is far more deadly than open rejection; it ignores Him. . . . In modern universities, as in modern society 'some think God exists, some think not, some think it is impossible to tell, and the impression grows that it does not matter.' . . . It is in this sense that the university today is atheistic. If in your organization, your curriculum, and your communal customs and ways of life, you leave God out, you teach with tremendous force that, for most people and at most times, He does not count; that re-

[15] Cf. Newman, *op. cit.*, "Religious truth is not only a portion, but a condition of general knowledge."

ligion is at best something extra and optional, a comfort for the few who are minded that way, but among the luxuries rather than the necessities of life. . . . Since it is the habit of the modern university to study all other subjects without any reference to theology at all, the obvious inference is that it does not 'admit a God' in any sense that is of practical importance. It is a fallacy to suppose that by omitting a subject you teach nothing about it. On the contrary you teach that it is to be omitted, and that it is therefore a matter of secondary importance. And you teach this not openly and explicitly, which would invite criticism; you simply take it for granted and thereby insinuate it silently, insidiously, and all but irresistibly. . . .

"In the assumptions governing curriculum and academic method, the universities today are implicitly, if not intentionally, hostile to the Christian faith and even to a liberal humanism." [16]

Let us be quite clear what is at stake here. Not sentimental loyalty to religion. What is at stake is, pure and simple, an issue of TRUTH—of fidelity to the Sovereign which all learning acknowledges as liege Lord.

V

We have said that the first revolution in American education was most clearly revealed in the curriculum—in the quiet displacement of religion from its earlier position as the keystone of the arch of truth to an inconspicuous, and incongruous, role as one stone among many, one subject, often an insignificant and ill-favored subject, among the multitudinous and ill-ordered assortment of intellectual delicacies which to-

[16] *The Crisis in the University*, pp. 55–56, 27. Copyright by The Macmillan Company and used with their permission.

gether make up the menu of the modern college curriculum. This change, we suggested, closely paralleled the alteration in the place of Christian Faith in the lives of most Americans— its gradual removal from unchallenged centrality to a secondary but still important status, and then to an incidental or peripheral concern. Would anyone question that that has in fact been the fate of religion in American culture in the past half century?

And we have noted striking, if tardy and sometimes half-hearted, attempts to restore meaning and unity to learning through curricular reform.

But the curriculum is only one factor in education, even when the most important. What we have to face is not simply defect in curricular construction; indeed, that is important only as a symbol of the whole educational process. The same considerations which would return religion to pivotal centrality in thought should restore it to regnant centrality in all of life. Here, our forebears were wiser than their children.

Our world cries pitiably for the fruits of Christian Faith, especially in today's youth who must drive a way through tomorrow's hazards and uncertainties—"firmer and stronger character, higher integrity, larger spiritual vision, unimpeachable and unshakable fidelity, what one of our foremost American statesmen keeps pleading for, 'a righteous and dynamic faith.' " The desired fruits *can* be had; but only from roots capable of producing them.

What is required—what alone might prove adequate—is revolution, conversion, an about-face, in both the assumptions and the goals of our living; and, likewise, of the training of our youth. Not the curriculum only, but every aspect of the philosophy and structure and spirit of education, cries for radical remaking.

IN SUMMARY

IN SUMMARY

WE TOOK our start from a comment by the late Archbishop of Canterbury on what he called "the most disastrous moment in the history of Europe—that period of leisure when René Descartes, having no claims to meet, remained for a whole day 'shut up alone in a stove.' "

Dr. Temple placed his playful yet pointed jibe at Descartes within the context of a comprehensive, profound and arresting interpretation of the history of human thought. Because this interpretation constitutes the setting, not the substance, of this notable volume of Gifford Lectures, it has been somewhat overshadowed by the massive theistic argument which it frames and, in my judgment, has received much less attention than it merits. The major contention of this small book rests squarely on the soundness of Temple's theory regarding the development of western thought; therefore, its importance for our study can hardly be exaggerated.

II

Dr. Temple's reading of history recognizes a dialectical pattern, with its familiar three phases—*thesis*, *antithesis*, and *synthesis*. The *thesis* represents the main line of advance. From time to time, when movement along that line has become stagnant and sterile, there arises a vigorous movement of *antithesis* which challenges the traditional and complacent assumptions of the thesis at every point. Ultimately, there succeeds a *synthesis* of reconciliation in which much of the truth of both thesis and antithesis is embraced. But—here is the most original and challenging teaching in Temple's exposition—the antithesis is always essentially a negative phase; its invaluable service is to criticize and correct. But it lacks creative and constructive power. The true direction forward is that of the *thesis*. And, after the salutary catharsis of a period of criticism and correction, advance is resumed by a return to the thesis, now purified and reformed by the power of the antithesis.

Let us hear this argument in Temple's own words:

"The 'thesis' formulates a *prima facie* view, which, because it is taken *prima facie*, has much of the quality of 'common sense.' It has that kind of guarantee that is provided by absence of sophistication. It is like the wisdom of the uneducated rustic—a wisdom which is the direct deposit of actual experience in a mind of which the balance has never been distorted. This wisdom has great limitations, but it is real wisdom, not cleverness.

"The 'antithesis' is born of the limitations of the 'thesis.' The 'thesis' is never a complete statement; there are aspects of the problem which it ignores. As men become conscious of these, they feel the need to assert them. . . . So it becomes necessary to make a new start from the assertion of these hitherto neglected aspects, or from a deliberate questioning of what has hitherto been unquestioned. So the 'antithesis' receives statement. As compared with the 'thesis' it is artificial, a thing consciously constructed; it may be defended without conspicuous ingenuity, but it is not likely to be a fount of wisdom.

"When the 'antithesis' has been worked out, and its shortcomings also have become apparent, the time is come for the 'synthesis.' This is not a mere average struck between the two. It is always a reassertion of the 'thesis' with all that has proved valuable in the 'antithesis' digested into it."[1]

III

Now, what is the application of this theory to our intellectual background? The *main line of advance* in western civilization has been that of the Graeco-Roman—Judaistic-Christian tradition whose two principal source streams sprang from wells deep in the early history of the Greek and Hebrew peoples, were enormously enriched and empowered in Greece's Golden Age and at the birth of Christianity, and merged in the early centuries of the Christian era. This Hellenistic-Christian tradition flowed steadily down the centuries until it became cluttered with accumulated refuse and congealed in sterile scholasticism in the later Middle Ages.

Then came the movement of *antithesis,* personified by Descartes. Like all antitheses, it was inevitable, and invaluable. But, like all antitheses, it was essentially negative and corrective; it lacked vital powers for origination of thought and cultural advance.[2]

That movement has now largely exhausted its vitality, and served its usefulness. The moment when the *synthesis* is due is upon us. But—if it is to be a true synthesis, it will not be a mere patching together of elements from thesis and antithesis. *Rather, in the perspective of later history, it will be discerned to be a return to the thesis—the main line of advance in western culture—corrected and purified by the influence of the Modern Era.*

[1] *Nature, Man and God,* pp. 58–59. Copyright by The Macmillan Company and used with their permission.
[2] We have already noted the extent to which developments in Europe which occupied nearly two millennia have, in the United States, been telescoped into roughly two centuries. See above, p. 44.

Here is Archbishop Temple's own account of the history:

"In the field with which we are now concerned the 'thesis' finds expression in various forms in the whole of ancient and of mediaeval thought. . . .

"During the fifteenth century many things were happening which tended to arouse the critical spirit. All tradition and the assurance associated with it was bound up with the Church. There was a scheme of thought embracing Theology, Metaphysics, Logic, Politics, Ethics and Economics. It was in itself coherent and close-knit; but Theology was the keystone of its arch, and the guardian of theological doctrine was the Church. . . . Meanwhile the spirit of Nationalism was developing. . . . A clash between the new Nationalism and the old Catholicism was inevitable. . . .

"The first actual breach came, as was natural and almost necessary, in the religious sphere itself. Europe was living by a system of tradition too narrow for it; the keystone of that system was the theology of a Church now seen to be corrupt. A breach was bound to come. But if the Church and its system were repudiated, what could take its place? If a man's thoughts and purposes were no longer to take their start from the only tradition available, where could they begin? And the only possible answer was 'with himself'. . . . So the modern movement was bound to be a movement of individualism. We owe to it the distinctive blessings of modern life, but also its distinctive ills. . . .

"The chief characteristic of the modern or post-Reformation period has been departmentalisation. The great enterprise of all-inclusive unity, which was characteristic of the Middle Ages, was progressively abandoned. . . . What has been the result for mankind? . . .

"Religion also had become departmentalised, and was by most people regarded as a 'private affair between a man and his Maker,' so that its main if not its only concern was with personal piety. . . . Art in like manner became incapable of permeating life with Beauty because it had adopted the principle of 'Art for Art's sake'. . . . Philosophy meanwhile has been left with the study of knowledge in general, and has been in preposterous disproportion occupied with the enquiry whether and how Knowledge may be possible at all. . . .

"The time is come, I am convinced, when we should learn to see the course of 'modern thought' up to date— that is, its course from about A.D. 1500 till near our own time—as one phase in a 'dialectical movement of thought'. . . .

"Return to the concrete richness and bewildering variety and still more bewildering interconnexion of actual experience must be the mode of deliverance from that false scent on which Descartes set the modern mind in its search for truth. . . .

"It is our task consciously and deliberately to construct a 'synthesis' of the classical and mediaeval 'thesis' with the modern 'antithesis,' and this in some fundamental respects will resemble the 'thesis' more closely than the 'antithesis.' But it will not leave the 'antithesis' unexpressed. . . ." [3]

IV

Analogies from individual life to social history are always tempting, though of limited validity. But there is an analogy here which is almost irresistible. It is a truism that the normal development of each person passes through three phases.

[3] *Op. cit.*, pp. 57–80, greatly abridged. Copyright by The Macmillan Company and used with their permission.

The first, a period marked by indoctrination in the accumulated wisdom of parents and society, carries the child until fourteen or fifteen years of age.

Then follows the brief but turbulent transition of adolescence, characterized by revolt against the "great tradition," the discovery of "new" worlds and "new" truths. This may last three or four years, until age nineteen or twenty.

But, if true maturity is achieved, it consists in no small part in a return to the well-worn paths, and the recovery of much which had been wholly discarded in "thoughtless youth"—a return to the main line of the "thesis" of youthful education, purified and corrected by the "antithesis" of adolescent revolt.

Substitute roughly a century for each year of individual life, and we have a striking parable of the pilgrimage of western culture during the Christian era. More particularly, all through these recent centuries—the "modern period"—the life of Western Man, and especially of the American people, has exhibited many features strangely familiar in youth's passage through adolescence.

If the analogy holds, another time of transition is upon us. Perhaps two World Wars within a quarter-century, and the threat of a third, sound the warning. The time is ripe for Western Man's "coming of age."

V

If this interpretation be sound, as I believe in main outline it is, we stand at the close of an epoch of criticism and correction, essentially negative in character, which began roughly with Descartes and has dominated the last three centuries. But we stand as children of that negative, one-sided and dying impulse. There can be no sound advance save through those whose whole outlook has been radically and thoroughly remade; that is, those who have been soundly converted to authentic religious faith. For what is demanded is reconstruction of almost every generally accepted assumption of our day, regarding the nature of human life, education and politics, the relation of emotion, reason and faith, the relation of the individual and the community, as well as the relation of God to His world and His creatures, and the role of religion in human fulfillment.

Let us be clear what is required. Not an uncritical return to ancient days and old ways. Not the slavish reproduction in this modern time of many familiar features of earlier philosophy and social organization. Not the rejection or loss of a single sound achievement of recent centuries. What is required is something at once far more fundamental, far more drastic and far more embracing—the recovery of the inherent principles which guided and empowered "the great tradition." More specifically, the reaffirmation of the organic unity of Truth, and therefore of true knowledge; of the interrelatedness and interdependence of the individual and society, of man and Nature, of the world and God, of this life and the Life Beyond; the worth of tradition as the bearer of accumulated truth and, therefore, the principal begetter of sound advance; above all—the genetic and sovereign principle of the Hebraic-Hellenic-Christian tradition—the restoration of religion to a position of necessary and unchallenged centrality; and the acknowledgment of the reality and regnancy of the Living God as the foundation of both learning and life.[4]

We may not see the full realization of the needed synthesis and the resumption of sound advance in our lifetime. In any event, it is important that we should grasp its meaning, and be made captive to its service. For that synthesis is the true destiny of education in our day.

[4] Cf. Temple: "The restoration of unity to man's experience depends mainly on securing at once the supremacy of Religion among human interests, and the true spirituality of Religion both in itself and in the mode of its supremacy." *Op. cit.*, p. 81.

RELIGION IN PUBLIC EDUCATION

RELIGION IN
PUBLIC EDUCATION

THE legality, as well as the propriety, of religious instruction in educational institutions supported by public funds stands today in serious question because of recent decisions of the United States Supreme Court, notably in the so-called "McCollum Case." In the interpretation of the basic law of the land, especially when the Supreme Court has spoken, the layman-in-the-law may be expected to maintain a discreet if unconvinced silence. But, in this instance, values of highest significance for the ordinary citizen are at stake. And if, as some foremost constitutional authorities maintain, the Court's decision is to be regarded less as a correct reading of the original intention of the Constitution and more as a reflection of what the Court believes to be the public interest today, it is incumbent upon the ordinary citizen to apprise himself of the issues involved, in order that he may use what opportunities are open to him to declare the "public interest" as he conceives it.

The official statement of the facts and decision in the McCollum Case are as follows: [1]

[1] *Advance Opinions*, "Illinois *ex. rel.* Vashti McCollum v. Board of Education of Champaign County," 333 U.S. 203 (1948), quoted in Edward S. Corwin, "The Supreme Court as National School Board," in *Thought*, Vol. XXIII, No. 91, December 1948, pp. 665ff. (reissued, in slightly revised form, in *Law and Contemporary Problems*, Duke University School of Law, Winter 1949 issue).

"A local board of education in Illinois agreed to the giving of religious instruction in the schools under a 'released time' arrangement whereby pupils, whose parents signed 'request cards,' were permitted to attend religious-instruction classes conducted during regular school hours in the school building by outside teachers furnished by a religious council representing the various faiths, subject to the approval and supervision of the superintendent of schools. Attendance records were kept and reported to the school authorities in the same way as for other classes; and pupils not attending the religious instruction classes were required to continue their regular secular studies.

"The Court held that this arrangement was in violation of the constitutional principle of separation of church and state, as expressed in the First Amendment and made applicable to the states by the Fourteenth Amendment, and accordingly that the state courts below had acted erroneously in refusing relief to the complainant, parent and taxpayer, against the continued use of school buildings for such religious instruction."

The relevant sections of the First and Fourteenth Amendments to the Federal Constitution, it will be recalled, read as follows:

"Article I. Congress shall make no law respecting an establishment of religion, or prohibiting the free exercise thereof . . ."

"Article XIV., Sec. 1. . . . No State shall make or enforce any law which shall abridge the privileges or immunities of citizens of the United States; nor shall any State deprive any person of life, liberty, or property without due process of law, nor deny to any person within its jurisdiction the equal protection of the laws."

The strictly constitutional issues involved in the Supreme Court's decision in this case are mainly two:

1. Is the Court correct in its interpretation of what the framers of the First Amendment intended when they forbade Congress to make any law "respecting an establishment of religion, or prohibiting the free exercise thereof"?
2. Is the Court correct in holding that the Fourteenth Amendment makes the prohibition of action *by Congress* respecting religion (in the First Amendment) applicable also to *state* and *local* public authorities?

Professor Edward S. Corwin of Princeton University, one of the most eminent living authorities on the history and meaning of constitutional law, holds that on both scores the majority decision of the Court was in error. Dr. Corwin summarizes his full and fully documented critique of the Court's decision in these words:

"In the first place the justification for the Court's intervention was most insubstantial. In the second place the decision is based . . . on a 'figure of speech,' the concept of 'a wall of separation between Church and State.' Thirdly, leaving this figure of speech to one side, the decision is seen to stem from an unhistorical conception of what is meant by 'an establishment of religion' in the First Amendment. The historical record shows beyond peradventure that the core idea of 'an establishment of religion' comprises the idea of *preference* (i.e., *that no public authority should give a preference to any religion or any denomination*); and that any act of public authority favorable to religion in general cannot, without a falsification of history, be brought under the ban of that phrase. Undoubtedly the Court has the right to make history, as it has often done in the past; but it has no right to *remake* it. In the fourth place, the prohibition on the establishment of religion by Congress is not convertible into a similar prohibition on the States, under the authorization of the Fourteenth Amendment, unless the term 'establishment of religion' be given an application which carries with it invasion of somebody's freedom of religion, that is, of 'liberty.' (I.e., *unless the 'released time' program of the Champaign schools involved an establishment of religion of such a nature as to deprive the plaintiff in the case of freedom of religion. . . . So far as the Fourteenth Amendment is concerned, States are entirely free to establish religions, provided they do not deprive anybody of religious liberty.*) Finally, the decision is accompanied by opinions and by a. mandate which together have created great uncertainty in the minds of governing bodies of all public educational institutions." [2]

Professor Corwin's judgment, it will be agreed, constitutes a considered, highly competent, and sweeping indictment. Few who examine the evidence with comparable care will consider it exaggerated.

II

As Dr. Corwin suggests, the mischief in this extraordinary dictum of the Supreme Court lies not alone in its invalidation of a particular plan of religious instruction in public schools, although it does jeopardize "released time" programs of religious education in the municipal schools of some 2,200 communities in all but two of the forty-eight states, and also closely analogous programs of religious teaching which have

---

[2] *Op. cit.*, p. 681. The two italicized passages in parentheses are quoted from earlier sections of Professor Corwin's article, p. 673 and pp. 677–678. The italics are his.

been firmly established for years in scores of state universities and colleges.[3] Its greater mischief is implicit in its misreading of the intention of the framers of the Constitution with respect to the role of religion in American life and to the more specific question of the relations of State and Church. The decision declares that the "released time" program in Champaign was "in violation of the constitutional principle of separation of church and state." In this and another recent decision,[4] the Court holds that the phrase in the First Amendment about laws "respecting an establishment of religion," when supplemented by the Fourteenth Amendment, forbids both National Government and State Governments to "pass laws which aid one religion, aid all religions, or prefer one religion over another." And the Court maintains that the intention of the First Amendment is to be discovered in a phrase of Thomas Jefferson's in a letter which he wrote to a group of Baptists in Danbury, Connecticut, in 1802, namely, to erect "a wall of separation between church and state."

As far as the threadbare phrase "separation of church and state" is concerned, Professor Corwin points out that, far from being a "constitutional principle" as the majority of the Supreme Court now assume, the Constitution itself does not contain the word "Church" or the word "separation," and the word "State" in the generic sense occurs only in Amendment II regarding the necessity of "a well-regulated militia . . . to the security of a free State." [5] The phrase has become so comfortably domesticated within our vocabularies and is so frequently employed as though it sprang from the lips of the Founding Fathers that it is important to be quite clear that it has no *constitutional* standing whatever, and that the attitude of the Founding Fathers must be discovered from

[3] See below, pp. 111–115.
[4] Everson v. Board of Education, 330 U.S. 1.
[5] Corwin, *op. cit.*, p. 668.

their own sayings and writings and not from this catch-all which has been erroneously read back into their minds.

What, then, was the attitude of the authors of the Constitution toward the place of religion in national life in general and education in particular, and toward the relations of State and Church, and what did they have in view in forbidding Congress to make any law "respecting an establishment of religion or prohibiting the free exercise thereof"? The names most frequently cited in support of the Supreme Court's recent interpretation are those of James Madison and Thomas Jefferson.

It is true that, in his later years, Madison developed an ardent advocacy of the "separation" of Church and State, even opposing the appointment of chaplains for Congress or for the Armed Forces. But his own original formulation of what subsequently became the First Amendment read as follows:

> "The civil rights of none shall be abridged on account of religious belief or worship, nor shall any national religion be established, nor shall the full and equal rights of conscience be in any manner, or on any pretext, infringed." [6]

What he had in mind is more fully set forth in this explanation:

> ". . . he apprehended the meaning of the words to be, that Congress should not establish a religion, and enforce the legal observation of it by law, nor compel men to worship God in any manner contrary to their conscience . . . if the word *national* was inserted before religion, it would satisfy the minds of honorable gentlemen. He believed that the people feared one sect might obtain a preeminence, or two combine together, and establish a re-

[6] *Annals of Congress*, I, 434.

ligion to which they would compel others to conform. He thought if the word national was introduced, it would point the amendment directly to the object it was intended to prevent." [7]

From these statements, it seems clear that, in Madison's view, the First Amendment was to apply only to the *national* government and that its purpose was to prevent that government from establishing *one particular form of religion*.

Jefferson was Ambassador to France at the time of the adoption of the First Amendment and therefore had no hand in its drafting. However, his authority is so repeatedly claimed in agreement with Madison and his attitude is so often currently defined as a determination to erect "a wall of separation between church and state" that it is worthwhile to be clear as to his viewpoint also, especially with respect to the role of religion in education. Jefferson did oppose the control of public education by any particular Church. But, setting forth his ideals for his own University of Virginia, he wrote.

"It was not, however, to be understood that instruction in religious opinion and duties was meant to be precluded by public authorities, as indifferent to the interests of society. On the contrary, the relations which exist between man and his Maker, and the duties resulting from those relations, are the most interesting and important to every human being, and the most incumbent on his study and investigation. The want of instruction in the various creeds of religious faith existing among our citizens presents, therefore, a chasm in a general institution of the useful sciences."

This "want" Jefferson proposed to overtake by encouraging the various sects to establish schools of divinity on the campus of the State University.

[7] *Ibid.*, cc. 730–731.

"Such an arrangement," he maintained, "would complete the circle of the useful sciences embraced by this institution, and would fill the chasm now existing, on principles which would leave inviolate the constitutional freedom of religion, the most inalienable and sacred of all human rights." [8]

At the same time, Jefferson envisioned that the Professor of Ethics in the University would "deal with the proof of the being of God and the divine authority of morals." [9]

In view of the importance attached to the views of these two great Virginians, it is interesting to observe that the Virginia Legislature postponed ratification of the First Amendment as unsatisfactory just because it *did not go far enough* to suit them:

". . . although it goes to restrain Congress from passing laws establishing any national religion, they [i.e., Congress] might, notwithstanding, levy taxes to any amount for the support of religion or its preachers; and any particular denomination of Christians might be so favored and supported by the general [i. e., national] government, as to give it a decided advantage over the others, and in the process of time render it powerful and dangerous as if it was established as the national religion of the country." [10]

It must always be recalled that, at the time of the framing of the Constitution and the addition to it of the Bill of Rights, *a particular religion,* one or another of the Christian sects, *was* in fact *established* in no fewer than five of the States.

[8] Saul K. Padover, *The Complete Jefferson,* pp. 957–958. Quoted by Corwin, *op. cit.,* from Justice Reed's dissenting Opinion in the McCullom Case, note 11. Most of the quotations in this section I owe to Dr. Corwin.

[9] Albea Godbold, *The Church College of the Old South,* pp. 178–179.

[10] Quoted in Corwin, *op. cit. (Law and Contemporary Problems),* p. 12 n.

There was no suggestion whatever that the First Amendment was to affect in any way those establishments; this in itself is adequate proof that it was directed solely toward action by the national Congress. Indeed, Professor Corwin reminds us that the word "respecting" in the phrase "respecting an establishment of religion" is ambiguous.

> "This is a two-edged word: it forbids Congress to pass any law *disfavoring* as well as any law *favoring* an establishment of religion . . . I suggest that the word 'respecting' was adopted as much to protect the *establishments* which then existed in five states—Massachusetts, New Hampshire, Connecticut, Maryland, and South Carolina —as to prevent Congress from setting up a national establishment." [11]

Dr. Corwin brings his own study of the views of the Founding Fathers to conclusion with this judgment:

> "I sum up Madison's and Jefferson's attitude, therefore, not as demanding that public-supported education should be exclusively secular and admitting no religious elements; *but that no public authority should give a preference to any religion or any denomination.* Preference, special advantage, for this, that or the other religion or denomination, was what they wished to rule out and what they thought had been ruled out by the First Amendment." [12]

He calls Justice Story to his support in this reading of the matter:

> "It was impossible, that there should not arise perpetual strife and perpetual jealousy on the subject of ecclesiastical ascendency, if the national government were

[11] *Op. cit. (Thought)*, p. 671.
[12] *Op. cit.*, p. 673. Italics his.

left free to create a religious establishment . . . Thus, the whole Power over the subject of religion is left exclusively to the state governments." [13]

Justice Story's interpretation finds even more explicit and impressive vindication in Cooley's authoritative work on Constitutional Law:

> "By establishment of religion is meant the setting up or recognition of a state church, or at least the conferring upon one church of special favors and advantages which are denied to others. It was never intended by the Constitution that the Government should be prohibited from recognizing religion—where it might be done without drawing any invidious distinctions between different religious beliefs, organizations, or sects." [14]

Reverting to the contention of the Supreme Court that the First and Fourteenth Amendments together forbid both National and State Governments to "pass laws which aid one religion, aid all religions, or prefer one religion over another," Professor Corwin, whose argument I have reproduced freely throughout this section, summarizes the teaching of history:

> "Ignoring the ambiguous first clause of the statement ['aid one religion'], my own conclusion is that historical data support its last clause ['prefer one religion over another'], but rule out its middle clause ['aid all religions']. In short, what the 'establishment of religion' provision of Amendment I does, *and all that it does, is to rule out any preference or discrimination which is based on religious grounds.*" [15]

[13] Joseph Story, *Commentaries on the Constitution*, #1879.
[14] T. M. Cooley, *Principles of Constitutional Law*, pp. 224–225.
[15] *Op. cit.*, p. 669. Italics his.

III

The general viewpoint among the founders of the Republic is well described in Justice Story's authoritative work:

> "Probably at the time of the adoption of the constitution, and of the amendment to it, now under consideration, the general, if not the universal sentiment in America was, that christianity ought to receive encouragement from the state, so far as was not incompatible with the private rights of conscience, and the freedom of religious worship. An attempt to level all religions, and to make it a matter of state policy to hold all in utter indifference, would have created universal disapprobation if not universal indignation . . ." [16]

It would be difficult to frame a more accurate and adequate summary not only of the attitude and intention of the Founding Fathers but also of both the principle and the practice of the American nation regarding the role of religion in national concern through the past century and three-quarters. At only one point does Justice Story's statement require modification. The multiplying diversity of religious faiths and, more particularly, the numerical increase of adherents of Judaism have put some restraint upon the special encouragement of Christianity.

The relations which have actually prevailed between government (whether national, state or local) and religion and Church throughout our national history, and which widely prevail today, should be matters of common knowledge. They stand at very distant remove from "a wall of separation." On the contrary, State and religion, even State and Church, have been and are intimately intermingled at all levels and in a variety of ways. The *practice* of the American people acting

[16] *Op. cit.*, #1874.

through their governments in this matter has been and is very close to the intention of the framers of the First Amendment as Professor Corwin understands them—aid to "all religions" without preference for "one religion over another."

Some of the ways in which the *national government* has shown its concern for *religion* are:

Setting apart of days for national Thanksgiving or prayer.
Provision of chaplains in both Houses of Congress.
Appointment of chaplains in all the Armed Forces of the nation.
Almost universal recognition of God and appeal for Divine assistance on the part of successive Presidents and leaders of government generally.

A few of the ways in which both *national* and *state governments* are directly involved in *relations with the Churches* are:

Appointment of chaplains for the Armed Forces.
Appointment of chaplains in penitentiaries, hospitals and other government-maintained institutions.
Specific exemption of ministers' residences from tax liability, and recognition of contributions to churches as deductible, on Federal and State personal income taxes.

Perhaps the most widely prevalent and significant way in which *state and local governments* take cognizance of *Churches* and grant them exceptional recognition is in:

The exemption of ecclesiastical property from taxation.

But the concern of these same agencies of the public for *religion* is most clearly and significantly revealed in the provisions many of them make for *instruction in religion* in their educational institutions at both school and college levels—precisely the area of our special interest and of the Supreme Court's recent interdiction.

IV

An impression is widespread and appears to be gaining in currency that, in the field of publicly supported education especially at the university level, an impassable "wall of separation" has always stood not only between State and Church but even between State and religion. It would be difficult to fabricate a more fanciful distortion of history or a grosser travesty of the present situation. What are the facts?

We have had occasion above to call attention to Thomas Jefferson's desire for religious instruction within the curriculum of the University of Virginia and for the presence of divinity halls of the various sects on the University's campus. But of course Virginia represented the extreme left wing in Colonial higher education in this respect. At the University of North Carolina, students were expected to stand examination each Sunday afternoon on the church service of that morning, on the Bible, or on some course in religion.[17] As late as 1893 at least, daily morning prayers were held at North Carolina. Required attendance at chapel, daily or Sunday or both, seems to have been the general rule in Middle Western State universities in their early years. The University of Michigan discontinued compulsory services of worship in 1871, the University of Illinois in 1894 and Purdue University in 1901. But as late as 1885, a student was expelled from the University of Illinois for non-attendance at required chapel and the courts upheld his expulsion. Eight state institutions (11.5% of those accredited) maintain compulsory chapel services today, while eleven others (15.7% of the total) hold voluntary chapel.[18]

When we turn directly to religious instruction within state

[17] Godbold, *op. cit.*, pp. 180–181.
[18] Merrimon Cuninggim, *The College Seeks Religion*, p. 133.

institutions, the record is even more impressive. An inquiry conducted in 1939 revealed that among 37 leading state universities (including those of California, Colorado, Connecticut, Florida, Illinois, Indiana, Iowa, Kansas, Kentucky, Louisiana, Maine, Massachusetts, Michigan, Minnesota, Missouri, Nebraska, North Carolina, Ohio, Oklahoma, Pennsylvania, South Carolina, Tennessee, Virginia, Washington, West Virginia, and Wisconsin), 22 or 59.5% offered courses in religion in their regular curricula, while an additional 8 gave academic credit for courses in religion taught by unofficial agencies near the university. Thus "the grand total for state institutions [under examination] at which religion is offered for credit, whether or not in the regular curriculum, is 30, or 81.1%." [19] As mentioned in Chapter IV above, a more comprehensive study conducted by Dr. Merrimon Cuninggim in 1941 of the 70 state institutions accredited by the Association of American Universities disclosed that 21 or 30% maintain departments of religion, 35 more offer courses in religion in other departments of the university, while 6 others give academic credit for classes taken in off-campus schools or colleges of religion. In brief, students in 62 of the 70 accredited state schools, almost 90%, have the opportunity to elect academically recognized instruction in religion.

Moreover, the evidence is conclusive that these numbers are steadily mounting.

"Each of the successive surveys since the first by Professor Charles Foster Kent in 1922–23 has shown steady increase in the number of colleges offering courses, a constant broadening in the range of courses, a raising of the standards of the teaching personnel, and increased enrollment of students. . . . The developments in the state colleges and universities started much later and moved more slowly than in the private or church-related col-

[19] Cuninggim, *op. cit.*, p. 297.

leges. Yet the growth has been steady and consistent. In the present postwar period the rate of growth has been greatly accelerated." [20]

I have already cited Dr. Shedd's supplementary testimony that "at least a dozen state colleges and universities have established chairs or departments of religion, officially sponsored and financed, since the last War." Reference was made earlier to the new and comprehensive Department of Religion at the University of North Carolina inaugurated in 1947, and of similar plans in other state institutions. The presently prevailing tendency can be suggested in this contrast: at the University of Oregon during the closing years of the nineteenth century, "formal religious exercises of any sort were frowned on, and even a college Y.M.C.A. was regarded with suspicion," [21] while in 1939 the University of Oregon instituted a Department of Religion.

The actual programs of religious instruction at state schools present an interesting variety both as to content and as to organization and sponsorship. Where departments of religion are found within the regular curriculum, they may deal largely or even exclusively with religion in its generic and universal meaning, or they may present the beliefs and practices of one or more of the faiths most widely professed in this country and among their own students; on the whole, the former of the two alternative philosophies outlined earlier appears to prevail. Courses in religion offered in other departments of the curriculum may bear such titles as "The Bible as Literature" or "The Psychology of Religion." Perhaps most interesting of all, and most significant for our present concern, are the arrangements in a dozen state schools whereby courses offered at "schools" or "colleges" of religion set up for this

[20] C. P. Shedd, op. cit., pp. 16–17.
[21] H. O. Sheldon, History of the University of Oregon, p. 63, cited in Cuninggim, op. cit., p. 83.

purpose on or near the university campus may be elected by the state institution's students with full academic credit. For example, while the law of the State of Michigan prohibits the use of state funds for "indoctrinational" religious courses, Michigan State College has established a department of religion for which teachers are furnished by the Catholic, Jewish, and Protestant student centers near by. The courses have full standing and the instructors are listed in the College's catalog and are considered members of its faculty. A slightly variant pattern is presented at the State University of Iowa, where for many years a well-equipped and highly regarded School of Religion has been maintained in association with the University though supported entirely by non-official funds. Since 1938, however, the University has assumed full responsibility for the administrative expenses of the School including the salary of its Director, involving expenditures from the University budget of $10,000 a year. Thus, in several instances, the *State* is in direct, active and apparently mutually satisfactory partnership with the *Church* in the provision of religious instruction for the former's pupils. The rigorous application of the Supreme Court's decision in the McCollum Case to higher public education would threaten if not invalidate present practice in 90% of the state universities and colleges of the land.

Nor do these facts regarding chapel services and religious courses exhaust the evidence of state concern for religion and the readiness of publicly supported educational institutions to give all possible aid to the Churches and other religious institutions. Among the 37 leading state universities in the 1939 study, while just under a third maintain institutionally sponsored chapel, over 56% hold special religious convocations under college auspices; 45.9% provide official religious leadership (Chaplain, Director of Religious Activities, etc.) at university expense; and over 40% subsidize voluntary student religious groups such as the Christian Associations. Dr. Cuninggim, to whose exhaustive and perceptive studies I am indebted for these figures, suggests the implications of the facts in these words:

> "The relative prominence in the tax-supported institutions of official positions of religious leadership, and the relative paucity of chapel and religious instruction, signify a deep concern expressing itself in a willingness to try new methods, coupled with retention of their older policy of neglect, formed in more hesitant days and distrustful of traditional procedures. . . . Thus the state colleges, eager to demonstrate their concern for religion in ways not suspect, have turned to newer techniques." [22]

Professor Shedd summarizes the present situation thus: "State universities are more concerned today about religion than they have been at any other time during the present century." [23]

V

In summary, the theory of "a wall of separation between church and state" as currently propounded, far from being a perpetuation of the national tradition, represents a novel innovation in direct contradiction to the conviction of our forebears and the established habits of the nation.

The authentic "American tradition" has been admirably set forth by Dean Weigle: [24]

> "Here in America we believe in the separation of church and state. It is a sound principle, but one that is much misunderstood. It means just what the phrase im-

[22] Op. cit., pp. 176–177.
[23] Op. cit., p. 5.
[24] "The American Tradition and the Relation Between Religion and Education," in Religion and Public Education; Proceedings of a Conference, American Council on Education Studies, February 1945, pp. 32–34.

plies—that church and state are mutually free. It means a separation of control, so that neither church nor state will attempt to control the other. But it does not mean that the state acknowledges no God, or that the state is exempt from the moral law wherewith God sets the bounds of justice for nations as well as for individuals. . . .

". . . America has no state church; but the American government is not godless. The American government favors no sect and fosters no sectarianism, but it is founded upon faith in God and it protects religion. The distinction between sectarianism and religion has been maintained in many decisions made by our courts. The Supreme Court of the United States has declared: 'The term religion has reference to one's view of his relations to his Creator and to the obligations they impose of reverence for His being and character and of obedience to His will. It is often confounded with the cultus or form of worship of a particular sect, but is distinguishable from the latter.' . . .

"There is nothing in the status of the public school as an institution of the state, therefore, to render it godless. There is nothing in the principle of religious freedom or the separation of church and state to hinder the school's acknowledgment of the power and goodness of God. The common religious faith of the American people, as distinguished from the sectarian forms in which it is organized, may rightfully be assumed and find appropriate expression in the life and work of the public schools."

VI

To those concerned, as every American citizen should be concerned, for the dignity of the Law and the confidence of the public in its official interpreters, an examination of the recent pronouncements by the Supreme Court on the legality of religious instruction in public education must be both disillusioning and disquieting. Dean Weigle has spoken strongly but not without full justification when he writes:

"The Court's interpretation of what the First Amendment meant to the founding fathers who propounded it and voted for it is untrue, a falsification of history produced by methods of handling evidence which would shame any competent graduate student. In its declaration of what the First Amendment means today, the Court is making law. That may be one of its functions; but the falsification of history with which it attempts to support the new interpretation can not command respect." [25]

Or, as Professor Corwin puts it, "Undoubtedly the Court has the right to make history, as it has often done in the past; but it has no right to *remake* it."

To those concerned, as every religiously minded American should be, for the undergirding and empowerment of public education through the insights and resources of religious faith, the Supreme Court's decisions present a direct challenge. The Supreme Court of the United States has been wrong more than once before. It has ways of correcting its own misreading of the law as well as of changing law whose established readings it feels to be obsolete.[26]

If there be any justification for the position the Court has taken up, it cannot be discovered in its faithfulness to his-

[25] "Freedom of Religion and Education" in *Christianity and Crisis*, Vol. X, No. 13, July 24, 1950, pp. 98–103.

[26] "The decision in the McCollum case is to be grouped with those high-flying *tours de force* in which the Court has occasionally indulged, to solve 'forever' some teasing problem . . . or to correct . . . 'a century of error.' In my opinion the Court would act wisely to make it clear at the first opportunity that it does not aspire to become, as Justice Jackson puts it, 'a super school board for every school district in the nation.'" Corwin, *op. cit.*, p. 683.

toric precedent but rather in its sensitiveness to what it believes are the realities of American life today. The secularization of the Supreme Court's interpretation of the Constitution
is one more reflection of the progressive secularization of
American life. And yet this drastic prohibition of the teaching
of religion in the publicly sponsored schools of the land comes
just at the moment when evidence is overwhelming, as indicated above, of a steadily mounting demand on the part of
the American public for increased provision of religious instruction for their sons and daughters in state-supported
higher education. This suggests that the present Supreme
Court is somewhat behind the times in its sensitiveness to
the public mind.

The rectification of the Court's error will be effected largely
through correction of its reading of what contemporary realities require. It lies within the power of the American people,
and it is their duty, to make clear that they continue to desire
for their children, as their forebears prevailingly did, the influence of religion in the schooling offered the youth of the
land in publicly maintained institutions; and that they desire
their national Constitution to be interpreted as its authors
intended, and as it has in fact been interpreted throughout the
nation's history, so as to make possible a wide variety of provision of religious instruction and religious worship in public
schools and colleges.

BIBLIOGRAPHY

BIBLIOGRAPHY

Allport, Gordon W., et al. *The Religion of the Post-War College Student.* New Haven: Edward W. Hazen Foundation. (Reprint: *Journal of Psychology*, 1948.)

Baillie, John. *The Mind of the Modern University.* University Pamphlets, No. 1. London: S.C.M. Press, Ltd., 1946.

Bellinger, Alfred R. *Religious Perspectives of College Teaching: In the Classics.* New Haven: Edward W. Hazen Foundation, n.d.

Brown, William Adams. *The Case for Theology in the University.* Chicago: University of Chicago Press, 1938.

Calhoun, Robert L. *The Place of Religion in Higher Education.* Hazen Pamphlets, No. 2. Haddam, Conn.: Edward W. Hazen Foundation, n.d.

Chalmers, Gordon K. *The Prerequisite of Christian Education.* Hazen Pamphlets, No. 20. New Haven: Edward W. Hazen Foundation, 1947.

College Reading and Religion: A Survey of College Reading Materials. New Haven: Yale University Press, 1948.

Conant, James B. *Education in a Divided World.* Cambridge: Harvard University Press, 1948.

Corwin, Edward S. "The Supreme Court as National School Board," in *Thought,* XXIII (1948), 665–683. (Reissued, in slightly revised form, in *Law and Contemporary Problems,* Duke University School of Law, Winter 1949.)

Cuninggim, Merrimon. *The College Seeks Religion.* New Haven: Yale University Press, 1947.

Donham, Wallace Brett. *Education for Responsible Living.* Cambridge: Harvard University Press, 1944.

Espy, R. H. Edwin. *The Religion of College Teachers.* New York: Association Press, 1951.

Fairchild, Hoxie N. *Religious Perspectives of College Teaching: In English Literature.* New Haven: Edward W. Hazen Foundation, n.d.

General Education in a Free Society: Report of the Harvard Committee. Cambridge: Harvard University Press, 1945.

Gilkey, Charles W. "The Place of Religion in Higher Education," in *Religion and the Modern World.* University of Pennsylvania Bicentennial Conference. Philadelphia: University of Pennsylvania Press, 1941.

Godbold, Albea. *The Church College of the Old South.* Durham: Duke University Press, 1944.

Greene, Theodore M., et al. *Liberal Education Re-examined*. New York: Harper & Brothers, 1943.

——. *Religious Perspectives of College Teaching: In Philosophy*. New Haven: Edward W. Hazen Foundation, n.d.

Harbison, E. Harris. *Religious Perspectives of College Teaching: In History*. New Haven: Edward W. Hazen Foundation, n.d.

Hay, Clyde Lemont. *The Blind Spot in American Public Education*. New York: The Macmillan Company, 1950.

Higher Education for American Democracy. A Report of the President's Commission on Higher Education. Vol. I. New York: Harper & Brothers, 1948.

Hutchins, Robert M. *Education for Freedom*. Baton Rouge: Louisiana State University Press, 1943.

——. *The Higher Learning in America*. New Haven: Yale University Press, 1936.

Jenkins, Daniel T. *The Place of a Faculty of Theology in the University of To-day*. University Pamphlets, No. 8. London: S.C.M. Press, Ltd., 1946.

Johnson, F. Ernest. "The Role of Religion in General Education," in *Teachers College Record*, LI (January 1950), 222–232.

Jones, Howard Mumford. *Education and World Tragedy*. Cambridge: Harvard University Press, 1946.

——. "Religious Education in the State Universities," in *Religion and Education*, ed. by W. L. Sperry. Cambridge: Harvard University Press, 1945.

Limbert, Paul M. ed. *College Teaching and Christian Values*. New York: Association Press, 1951.

Livingstone, Sir Richard. *On Education*. New York: The Macmillan Company, 1945.

——. *Some Thoughts on University Education*. Hazen Pamphlets, No. 23. New Haven: Edward W. Hazen Foundation, n.d.

Lowry, Howard. *The Mind's Adventure*. Philadelphia: Westminster Press, 1950.

Maritain, Jacques. *Education at the Crossroads*. New Haven: Yale University Press, 1943.

Miller, R. C. *The Clue to Christian Education*. New York: Scribners, 1950.

Moberley, Sir Walter. *The Crisis in the University*. New York: The Macmillan Company, 1950.

Morison, Samuel E. *The Founding of Harvard College*. Cambridge: Harvard University Press, 1935.

Nash, Arnold S. *The University and the Modern World*. New York: The Macmillan Company, 1943.

Nason, John W. "Religion in Higher Education: A Program of Faculty Consultations," in *The Educational Record*, XXVII (1946), 422–432.

Newman, John Henry. *On the Scope and Nature of University Education*. London and Toronto: J. M. Dent and Sons, Ltd., 1915.

Oldham, Joseph H. *Christian Education: Its Meaning and Mission*. Pamphlet, privately printed, 1931.

O'Neill, Milton. *Religion and Education under the Constitution*. New York: Harper & Brothers, 1949.

Outler, Albert C. "Colleges, Faculties and Religion," in *The Educational Record*, XXX (1949), 45–60.

Princeton University. *Plan of Study Leading to the Degree of Bachelor of Arts*. Princeton, N. J.: Princeton University, 1945.

Schneider, Herbert and Carol, ed. *Samuel Johnson, President of King's College, His Career and Writings*. Vol. IV. New York: Columbia University Press, 1929.

Shedd, Clarence P. "The Agencies of Religion in Higher Education," in *Religious Education*, XXXVIII (1943), 287–298.

———. *The Church Follows Its Students*. New Haven: Yale University Press, 1938.

———. *Proposals for Religion in Postwar Higher Education*. Hazen Pamphlets, No. 11. Haddam, Conn.: Edward W. Hazen Foundation, 1946.

———. *Religion in the American State Universities: Its History and Present Problems*. Unpublished manuscript.

———. *Religion in the State University*. Hazen Pamphlets, No. 16. New Haven: Edward W. Hazen Foundation, 1948.

———. *Two Centuries of Student Christian Movements*. New York: Association Press, 1934.

Shuster, George N. *Education and Religion*. Hazen Pamphlets, No. 10. Haddam, Conn.: Edward W. Hazen Foundation, 1945.

Smith, Elliott H. ed. *Education for Professional Responsibility*. New York: Carnegie Press, 1948.

Tead, Ordway. *Toward First Principles in Higher Education*. Hazen Pamphlets, No. 19. New Haven: Edward W. Hazen Foundation, 1947.

Temple, William. *Nature, Man and God*. London: The Macmillan Co., Ltd., 1934.

Tewksbury, Donald G. *The Founding of American Colleges and Universities Before the Civil War*. New York: Teachers College Bureau of Publications, 1932.

Thomas, George F. *Religion in an Age of Secularism*. Princeton, N. J. Princeton University, 1940.

Van Dusen, Henry P. "Religion and Education," in *Modern Education and Human Values*. Pittsburgh: University of Pittsburgh Press, 1947.

———. *Trends in the Philosophy of Higher Education*. Philadelphia, Pa.: The Princeton Club of Philadelphia, 1946.

Weigle, Luther A. "The American Tradition and the Relation between Religion and Education," in *Religion and Public Education*, pp. 26–34. (Conference on Religion and Public Education, Princeton, 1944.) Washington, D. C.: American Council on Education, 1945.

Whitehead, A. N. *Nature and Life*. Chicago: University of Chicago Press, 1934.

———. *Science and the Modern World*. New York: The Macmillan Company, 1925.

Williams, J. Paul. *The New Education and Religion*. New York: Association Press, 1945.

Yale College. Report of the Committee on the Course of Study (Adopted by Faculty, Spring 1945). Unpublished report.

INDEX